Walking Into Oneness

Harjinder Kaur Chohan

ParamAmarSaran Sat-Deep
Supreme Eternal Surrender in Truth to the LIGHT
This is a foundation set to empower the Divine Light to lead us to our Truth

All voluntary contributions
welcome with an open heart
& soul in one LIGHT to:
ParamAmarSaran Sat-Deep
or Mrs H K Chohan
11 Pennine Way
Nuneaton
Warks
CV10 8PW

heel2heal2whole@yahoo.co.uk

1st WORLD
PUBLISHING

Walking into Oneness

Harjinder Kaur Chohan

© Harjinder Kaur Chohan 2009

Published by 1stWorld Publishing
P. O. Box 2211, Fairfield, Iowa 52556
tel: 641-209-5000 • fax: 866-440-5234
web: www.1stworldpublishing.com

First Edition

LCCN: 2009924390
SoftCover ISBN: 978-1-4218-9079-1
HardCover ISBN: 978-1-4218-9078-4
eBook ISBN: 978-1-4218-9080-7

Everything written in this pilgrimage was an experience. I have no knowledge about any Religious scripture. I am only writing from the inner deep experience I have felt from the twelve monthly shabads which I was given from Within to chant during this journey. So I ask for forgiveness from anyone, who has been offended by anything written here. Also remember truth changes in every moment. This written journal is only my truth from that moment in the past, not necessarily my truth in the Now.

The first time I talked to God was when my Christian neighbour told me about the tree of heaven in her front garden. Knowing its name I believed it was absolutely true. Underneath that tree I wrote my first piece of poetry; from then on, poetry became therapeutic bliss for me. Also underneath the tree I said many prayers for a sister. She was born after my two brothers and was eight years younger than me. I sang to her; she was very alert. It was when she was a few months old we found out she was deaf. I felt it was my responsibility to listen for her, to describe everything to her. I woke up each morning feeling so lucky to hear the birds singing, to hear the wind rustling, and children screaming on their bikes. I felt so lucky to hear my mum's voice calling me and, most of all, to hear my sister's laughter. Her laughter was like that of a flower blooming, its petals opening with the same vibration as pure innocence.

I learnt so much from her. I just had to look at the milk bottles and she would take them outside; just one gesture and she always knew. She could read people and yet I could read no one.

How would my sister ever know how grateful I was for all my senses? I had to show her, and thus my journey in spirit began. At first it felt a duty to show this joy, love, and gratitude, but soon the joy of life could not stop smiling, laughing, dancing, and singing through me. It became my nature.

In the February of 1990 I had an accident whilst standing on a metal folding chair which collapsed; I fell backwards, fracturing my back in three places in my lumbar vertebrae. I screamed; the pain was so great that I thought I went into a coma, because the place I was in was total peace and emptiness, yet I could hear everything around me. That year there was an ambulance strike so my husband pulled my floppy body down the stairs to put me in the car. At hospital everyone thought I must be bruised, only in the morning, when he saw the X-ray, did the doctor alarm the others and I had injections to ease the pain. I had to be so still; every tiny movement caused so much pain. That morning, right there inside the pain, there were moments of complete stillness and darkness. In this darkness I heard a voice. This gentle voice I used to hear as a child, only as a child I thought it was God's voice speaking from outside. Now this voice was from within. It asked softly, 'What have you done for your self?' I started telling it all the things I had done for others. It asked me the same question again, 'And what have you done for your self?' I started going on and on again about all I had done for my family, my husband's family, my children, and others. When it asked me the same question once again in its sincere gentleness, I realised 'I' disappeared and there was just silence left.

Harjinder Kaur Chohan

My doctor wanted me to have the disability label and money, but I decided not to sign the paper; something inside me did not see me that way. I even let go of the wheelchair and flopped on the floor. My eldest son said, 'Mum, I will be your legs.' Something in me collapsed as I had a vision of him pushing my wheelchair and me taking away his childhood. His love, his offering gave me the strength to have faith in myself. If only I could just learn to be strong, to do things for myself. Without the use of my back, my arms had no strength. I lay on a wooden board for nearly nine months, until I slowly started to walk and drive. Gently, I became strong.

In January of 2007, after receiving unsettling news, I heard my Higher Self whisper, 'You need to start a pilgrimage.' Immediately my ego asked, 'Where to? India?' as if it had spoken, and the voice replied softly 'You don't need to go anywhere; start from here, go to a local lake early in the Amrit Vela[1], nothing else should change; it should be an addition to your working life.'

I was given a few clear instructions which my husband and I had to follow. I realised that my whole being did not question this; it just surrendered to this Truth. When we surrender, we open and empty everything we ever thought we knew, and in that space grace flows. In the absence of

[1] The Amrit Vela are the ambrosial hours before dawn, when Sikhs do their *sadhana, jap ji sahib,* chant the True Name, and contemplate His Glorious Greatness. Giving one-tenth of the day, two and one-half hours each morning, cleanses and purifies at a deep level.

ego, the questioner falls away, the consciousness rises to transform the karma to dharma, giving full clarity to the sole purpose of our destiny in that moment. This book is a distillation of my husband and my evolutionary growth together as a family.

We were to keep a daily personal diary of our observations, understandings, and lessons from life and nature. For forty days my husband was to make five *gypatties*[2] for the birds on the lake and I was to distribute them. He was also to cook for me and I had to wait for my food and not just make it for myself. We were to wake up as early as possible and chant prayers whilst walking to the lake and pray there, sharing our realisations. We were to look into each other's eyes and say, 'Thank you' for five things about each other.

[2] Gypatties - Indian bread made from flour and water on a hot pan. At times I will quote it as 'bread', as it is universally known.

1 January. Day One

When my husband and I went to the lake there were five swans next to us eating the bread with mallards, Canada geese, and flocks of different birds.

It felt odd offering the bread to the birds when I had no part in the making of it.

Learning:

The Lord gives, yet there are many who squander—fighting, cheating, and biting to receive what they think they should have by right. Be like some of the birds, who stay away, in faith and contentment waiting, trusting the Lord, knowing of his abundance.

2 January. Day Two

Before dawn it was chilly and windy, I did the 'I am'[3] meditation on the way to the lake. There were no birds there;

---

[3] 'I am' Meditation is a spiritual practice technique where you identify that everything you see, hear, or feel with the senses is **You**. You become interwoven and integrated with body, mind, intellect, heart, and soul and with what you say you are. For example, when I see the tree, I say 'I am the tree', 'I am the breeze', 'I am the rain', and 'the bird' etc. You keep repeating 'I am' until the words fade and you become ONE source.

the water lashed and splashed against the banks and over the wooden fishing platform jutting into the lake.

Waiting to be given food makes me feel like a monk with a begging bowl in my hands. A sacred trust embraces my body and a deep humility rises from within. The discipline of having to wait to be given food, instead of being able to reach for it from habit, was like a rebirth of consciousness. Contentment, trust, and faith were being nurtured and opened from within. In gratitude and patience my body was waiting to be fed. The physical hunger during this pilgrimage period could not be satisfied. The waiting for my family to arrive home from work seemed an eternity. My physical hunger knew there was nothing it could do, so it beckoned me to sit and be patient. A deep and loving honouring of my family's anticipated return opened and bloomed from within. I truly honoured and appreciated them as I had not recognised before.

Learning:

Be awake. The Lord gives abundantly, yet our conscious mind does not always recognise this. In the early hours of the morning the ego (I mind) is sleeping. The eternal unconscious being is always awake, open in humility, vibrating in God consciousness. The world is at peace. When we trust like the birds, we will be fed, nurtured in true abundance. It's not just the ones we see that God feeds through us, but also the ones we do not see, such as the fish beneath the waves. There is a lot that is unseen.

Harjinder Kaur Chohan

Open the eye of wisdom; see with the third (intuitive) eye, as well as the physical eye.

3 January. Day Three

I listened to my husband read the prayer of contentment and peace (Sukhmani Paath[4]) before we went to the lake where there was a cold breeze. We climbed over the fence and walked through the slushy mud and sat on the wooden platform where the cold water slopped and slapped against us, soaking all, including our feet, legs, and coat. The sometimes veiled, silver moon, full and bright, seemed to smile. The silhouetted trees appeared from the darkness as dawn broke with a lone star. As my husband gave me the *gypattie* pieces and I finished throwing them, I watched a large black bird flying past call everyone to awaken both physically and spiritually. The waves continued in the rhythm of their dance of life. Our attention was captured by a shimmering, arrow-like shaft of light arching, shining so brightly, profoundly, and majestically. It took my breath away. I understood the mystical and

[4] This prayer was a composition of Guru Arjun dev Ji, the fifth guru of the Sikhs. It is said that the Guru ji wrote it in reply to a request from a disciple who was suffering from physical pain and mental torture. Once listening and meditating to this prayer, the disciple became healthy, innately calm, and blissful.

magical message of God's love, and its splendour awakened my deepest humility and reverence. I felt as if I were the richest person in the world. I had seen a shooting star. My spirit soared, enveloped in the Lord's love. It seemed like a different place, time, and dimension. We were human and spirit in the unity of God's eternal love.

Learning:

My husband observed a trinity where he felt that there was the Creator, Distributor, and Receiver. He had made the *gypattie;* I distributed it to those whom it fed. The Lord is the Creator, using his angelic messengers and us to manifest his bounty. According to the choices we make and the deeds we do, we cocreate with God our destiny. When we walk on the path of light and Truth, we become soaked in the abundance of love. We are sleepwalkers and need to awaken to receive this pure, holy awareness in the golden, ambrosial hour before the hustle of the day begins.

I saw the rushing waves greet and splash the bank, spraying and reuniting with the Oneness of the lake. This metaphor of our life on earth is like the arching spray in air before it reunites with the Oneness of the eternal life and God consciousness. Our emotions are linked with the phases of the moon, as are tides and for women, their menstrual cycles. Our emotions bubble like chemicals in the test tube of our body; they long for rebirth and freedom. When we observe from a distance, not personalizing the emotions that we experience, we are freed from the need to judge, blame, and victimise ourselves and others. Fear, doubt, judgement, blame, and victimisation have caused us to abdicate our responsibilities for our life choices. We blame others so to not accept our own responsibilities. When we become entangled, we cannot see the bigger picture or embrace these emotions with unconditional love, knowing that they are carrying us on the path to freedom.

4 January. Day Four

It was all so calm, yet my mind kept jumping from one meditation technique to another. I did not hear the prayers fully, I felt my husband was hurrying and not say-ing the words clearly, or was this just my lack of being present in the moment? My body was unsettled. Eventually peace and stillness came as my being opened into the yoga posture (*guyan mudra*)[5].

My husband observed that the waters were calm and as we repeated the prayer in the name of the Lord, our minds came to peace. There was an immense joy within me and a deep love for all the abundance we share. Our intense joy from the meditation continued on our homeward journey with chanting this month's prayer. We were totally uplift-ed by this peace.

Learning:

The moon was full, blessing us with light, guiding us through the slippery mud on this calm morning. I realized our physical bodies are like the bread floating on the water, before we also disintegrate and become one with our eternal self. In its pure state the water represents our soul, its very essence, connected to everything in universal creation. This permanence is more important than worrying about the temporary that will fade, as do our problems and life challenges.

[5] Guyan Mudra-as used in Kundalini yoga
From the book *Transitions to a Heart Centered World* by Guru Rattana, Ph.D

 **GUYAN MUDRA:** The tip of the thumb touches the tip of the index finger, stimulating knowledge and ability. The index finger is symbolized by Jupiter, and the thumb represents the ego. Guyan Mudra imparts receptivity & calm.

 **ACTIVE GUYAN MUDRA:** The first joint of the index finger is bent under the first joint of the thumb, imparting active knowledge.

Kundalini Yoga, "Mudras," http://www.kundaliniyoga.org/mudras.html

Harjinder Kaur Chohan

5 January. Day Five

We awoke later than intended, but it was still dark. I had been coughing during the night. The morning prayer and meditation came and went with my consciousness. Sometimes my mind observed the sensations in my body (*vipassana* meditation)[6], then it would concentrate on my third eye, my navel, and later my breathing. I observed peace between each breath.

I surrendered. Sometimes I was the observer perceiving all of it—the many different ways my mind ceased its restless tide. Chatter silenced. With closed eyes I drank the water that had absorbed the pure love and light from the prayers. The light was intense in my third eye. It illuminated a scintillating cross of light, strong as a silver sword. This awareness told me the water was holy; I should drink it holding the glass with my two hands cupped. This holy water was like matrimony, binding all this that I am to the light of the Lord. I felt so weightless, and my body and soul bowed in humility; I wanted to remain in this connectedness forever. I could see the molecules of light throughout my being as I scanned my body. The lumps of darkness and the blocks were slowly melting as I floated in the awareness of everything.

---

[6] *Vipassana* is a way of self-transformation through self-observation. *Vipassana,* which means to see things as they really are, is one of India's most ancient techniques of meditation. Rediscovered by Gotama Buddha more than 2500 years ago and taught by him as a universal remedy for universal ills.

On the walk my mind tried to compare the light. I observed my mind trying to talk to me and did not engage with it. I continued with my 'I am' meditation. Towards the end of the walk, I rarely heard what came after 'I am'; I had become that which I observed. There was so much peace in whatever I was; this peace was too great for my mind's intrusion.

At the lake, I watched the birds eat only when they were hungry. From this I was reminded I had often eaten for eating's sake—through the habitual pattern of greed rather than need. The discipline of having to be fed is becoming easier as I am surrendering. My husband is becoming relaxed and beginning to enjoy food preparation.

My husband confessed how hard he found it to sit for the prayers in the beginning, but now he could sit cross-legged for longer periods and his mind was at peace. He told me a Hindu story about Krishan, Arjan, and Dospathi. They had invited a low-caste person to their home for a feast. Dospathi had made a meal and the bell chimed more quietly than usual. Whilst the man was eating he mixed all the different, delicious dishes that had been prepared with elegance and style. This made Dospothi very angry. She thought, 'Low caste people do not know how to eat with manners!' Later when Krishan asked her why the bell chime was so quiet, Dospothi realised she had served with anger in her heart. This made her feel small within herself and she walked in penitence, barefoot to the man's home to invite him again. This time she prepared the food with purity, happiness, and gratitude. With a clear mind of love the bell chimed louder than ever. The man had sensed Dospathi's disapproval on the initial visit; likewise, our thoughts and emotions ripple out from us, touching and affecting others.

My husband realised you cannot judge a person by his status or how he behaves. The low-caste man had been Dospathi's teacher. We should open our hearts and appreciate our abundance with gratitude. It is important to know that the caste system is only a man-made separation.

Upon arriving home from the lake, I smelt a fragrance of flowers. I asked my husband if he could smell them too. He replied that because of his cold he could not smell anything. For me, this essence was so strong, so warm, so welcoming, and so peaceful. It was like being in an aromatic garden. How blessed am I?

Learning:

The lake's muddy path made us slip and slide. Near footprints I observed a pile of shit. I must have walked through this many times to get to the platform. This enabled me to realise whilst walking in darkness, I could not see my own 'shit' that I had habitually created. Before our conscious awakening, we are all surrounded by darkness. In this darkness we walk through the 'shit' (condemnation of the mind), thus moving further away from the Lord.

When we become closer to the Lord in prayer, meditation, or any other means, although we are surrounded by darkness, the light within unites us with everything. Even the 'shit' becomes good, clean, and pure. In reality it is only what we have physically eaten. It is purer than the mind that plants crazy thoughts that lead to lies, war, famine, disease, murder, crime, hatred, and so fourth.

When we arrived at the lake, my husband observed one bird snatch a piece of bread from amongst the flock trying to feed. He realised that when people work hard for their possessions, others can feel envious. One should not look at another's belongings; who knows how honestly and with what integrity they were gained. Be content with the purity of what one has. We went through a process where we recognised how many times we had both done this in the past. He admitted that in the past he had wanted more money, more possessions—to be like others—and had become frustrated by apparently having less than they did. I admitted that my mind, in the past, had also been upset at times and wondered why, when I seemingly worked so hard, others appeared to have so much more with apparent ease.

I realised that another's possessions do not reflect their happiness, inner richness, or how much they have struggled beneath the surface. No matter how many material possessions we have, we still often feel separated from the support, love, and peace within. We need to appreciate the differences that unite us all in the diversity of creation. We separate ourselves, in our unconscious choices, from unity and Oneness by the illusion of the need for status and possessions.

6 January. Day Six

Learning:

Let your whole body light up with love, peace, and wonder. Sing from your heart, watch through the observer, dance to the beat of life, be present to everything you touch, and surrender your mind to the mystery. Put all thoughts into a bucket and empty them into the well of liberation. Wake up! Do not take anything for granted. Be grateful for every moment. Be present to now. Everything is calling to focus within on the light, not on the darkness or limitations of the commentator in the mind. The commentator can never be happy... Be the light. Experience the divine love of God within.

7 January. Day Seven

Whilst listening to this month's prayer, we discussed it with my brother-in-law and observed that where the five sins of ego exist, the Lord is absent; they cannot co-exist, as there can be only one or the other. **This is our choice.** Who is it to be, the Creator or the ego?

During our walking *satsang* (where Truth speaks), my husband told me a humorous story from when he was eight years old, about a lady who had returned from England to India in 1965. In delight she told everyone her experiences. 'England is an amazing place! It is a magical world! My daughter took me to a shop in the town, where she pressed a button. Guess what? We were taken to a place where there was meat; it smelled awful.' (She was a vegetarian!) 'My daughter pressed another button and everywhere there were clothes of all kinds, a different world of colour, styles, and sizes. Again she pressed the button and there were shoes, another button and there was jewellery, then food of all different kinds. Can anybody imagine— just with a press of a button?'

It was a lift and all the different floors in a department store. This reminded me of the first time I got close to an automatic door that opened for me. I was wowed by this experience. It happened again and again, whilst on another occasion I waited for the door to open and had not read the sign that said 'Push!'

Harjinder Kaur Chohan

It also reminded me of the different dimensions of time and space we go through when we are attuned. When we press a TV channel, it switches to that channel; likewise, when we meditate, we tune ourselves into a higher frequency and greater consciousness. There are places of higher and lower frequencies, as there are many varying levels of human consciousness.

I feel as if I am living in three different dimensions: the spiritual eternal world (Amrit Vela), this life's reality with its challenges and karmas, and then the dream world. It is amazing to be part of this embrace of trinity where two worlds of form, name, and concept come and go in the one ocean of space in which they dance. In the ambrosial hour one awakens and becomes aware of the illusions of the two sleeping states. Gently, subtle and strong illusions weaken their hold on us.

Learning:

Like telephone poles with their thin wires connect the homes to the exchange, we are all connected to each other in the divine consciousness. In openness, Truth, and pure love we heal the world, raising the consciousness so as to penetrate the lies, illusions, and the dimensions of time and space.

The swans dabbling with the food could only eat what they could reach in that moment, whilst I became aware that I fill my shopping bags and cupboards with more than I need in the now. We store up possessions and hoard them, displaying them for status and discarding them thoughtlessly, creating waste and scarcity. The beak that harvests the food nourishes the bird for survival. Our hands can carry nourishing food to our mouths or poison us with junk food, alcohol, drugs, and cigarettes. Our mouths habitually open, chew, and swallow whatever they are given. From the contentment of the birds we need to learn to feed ourselves with conscious, loving gentleness. I need to stop abusing my body by eating too much and using my mouth as a rubbish bin, just for the momentary pleasure of the tastes on my tongue.

My husband observed that the swans did not eat the dry bread from the surface of the lake; they saturated it before swallowing. We learned that when we take more than we need, we are constantly looking outside of what we already have, ignoring and hindering the natural flow of energy coming into our lives. This constant search is in the hope that when we finally have whatever we are ostensibly looking for, we will feel peace and self worth. This fantasy, loving what we don't yet have, overrides the present energy of abundance which already exists. Loving what we have in the present moment stops the search and all peace arrives instantly from the stillness which has always been inherent within. We have looked and searched fruitlessly outside ourselves, whilst all we need to do is look within and shed the onion-like layers to reveal the diamond in the heart of our being.

Harjinder Kaur Chohan

8 January. Day Eight

There is so much significance to the colour red. The berries in winter on the holly are red; our blood is bright red. Many nationalities and faiths, such as the Sikhs, Hindus, and Welsh, get married in red. The face of happiness is red (*laal chera* refers to the face of bliss on one who is enlightened); fire and lava is partly red. I realised that the sunrise and sunset brought beautiful reds to the beginning and end of the day. With the birth and death of each day, we are given the opportunity to make new choices towards our awakening. The colour red is permanent; it is the symbol of love, light, and warmth. Red is the colour of the base chakra, which represents the powerful physical energy that earths us to this planet. Red symbolizes creation and life.

Three cygnets, with their big brown breasts, came right up beside us, but did not eat the bread. They also watched the light shine from the platform across the lake, as if the light was a silver, dazzling ladder into holiness. It felt as if the light was beckoning us, with deepness of love, to follow this inward journey outward-bound to the bridge that united our consciousness to God consciousness.

Learning:

At the lake there was a line of reflected moonlight dancing, scintillating on the surface of the water whilst everything around it was in darkness. I was reminded the path of light is straight, clear, simple, and illuminating. When we are on its path, we are protected, loved, and lit from within. It is effortless, for it is a straight path.

9 January. Day Nine

The force of the wind was pushing us when we went to the lake. On the way I saw a tree with ivy clinging and covering the bare trunk and branches. One big branch has hung from the middle trunk for the past week, holding on, to remain a part of the whole. Like this, the Lord tries to save us all. When the branch will finally fall, if it stays by the tree it will rot into the ground, feeding the roots underground with its recycled nutrients. Likewise, the Lord is always taking care of us, even when we try to cut our branches from the trunk of life itself. We are never alone on the path to the Truth.

The trees swayed in the breeze; the waves drummed against the banks, dancing and cresting. The breeze through the branches became the shakers, the wind whistled in the air flutelike, and the symbols crashed as the waves slapped the platform. The ripping, howling wind sang the songs of grace. Nature orchestrated my chanting.

I acknowledged that all life is ordered—created to flourish

in every kind of environment—completing this interdependent, wonderful web of creation. We watched the lake water returning the banks' soil nutrients to the water, enriching all of its aquatic life, whilst simultaneously providing water to create another rich habitat. Seasons pass as part of this game, with a time for sowing and a time for reaping all part of nature's divine cycle of life. The wind of change becomes nature's broom, sweeping away the old in preparation for the new. The dance of life is like a game of chess.

Learning:

Our physical dance of life is when we live our lives by going to work, raising children, cleaning, and so forth, as part of our survival. However, we often use our external movements to avoid looking into ourselves to develop our spiritual growth. This creative energy is powered by the soul's wish to move inwards, reuniting with God's unconditional love and light. It is said that when you take one step towards the God within, that God takes 1001 steps towards you. Thus we are all given the choice of whether we follow the spiritual journey, whether we overcome the many obstacles and challenges that will test the sincerity of our will to reunite with the almighty Oneness of the God Self, where will dissolves and becomes one.

10 January. Day Ten

On this grey morning of pilgrimage, the pitter-patter of the raindrops dancing, massaging, and tickling my face made me laugh—lifting my spirit as I chanted the prayer. Yesterday the wind had dried and moved everything and today the life-giving, refreshing rain washed and purified creation. All weather and seasons are part of the divine cycle of life.

Our first major challenge was my discovery of a financial issue between a close member of my family and I, which this family member had been hiding from me for the duration of our relationship. I was shaken to the core, questioning my very being and integrity.

11 January. Day Eleven

It was a dark and windy morning as day broke; we had to lean into the wind to walk up to the corner. As soon as we turned, the lightened wind reminded me of a metaphor; when we walk through adversity and embrace the obstacles, the resistance melts.

Our two black coots bobbed up and down on the wind-roughened water that also soaked my lower body and feet.

Harjinder Kaur Chohan

I totally surrendered to the situation and felt untouched by the cold, wet, and darkness. In that total surrender, it was all part of God's breath (embrace). Whist walking, I needed to accept my husband's hand along the slippery path so neither of us fell, and I found that gentle love had a healing power.

I did not know how this close relative had incurred these debts over so many years and kept silent about them. Were these the total debts, and how could I truly trust this relative? Then I realised that **love is trust.**

I felt untouched by life's dramas, illusions, and even money. I knew I could survive and would have all that I need; there was nothing else that I would ever want. What is given in Truth carries uplifting energy, light, and joy and is worth its weight in gold.

Learning:

As I walked, my drenched coat made me realise that I was carrying the cold weight of yesterday's discovery. Yet we habitually and unconsciously carry the weight of karma, which we have produced by the actions we take and the thoughts we carry. If we could see and feel the weight and consequences of the lies, debt, and negative energy, we would want to cut the cords before they become enmeshed and out of control.

12 January. Day Twelve

It was a less breezy and mild morning. Like my mind, the waves on the lake seemed to want to escape their confines; but as the water returned to itself, both it and I surrendered deeply.

Today my coat felt warm and dry, but my shoes were cold and they brought me back into the moment.

Learning:

I realised when we give in to our ego and senses, we give in to our desires, which haunt, pollute, and imprison us. The five senses desire stimulation; for example, the eyes desire beauty, the ears desire praise and music. The senses feed the ego mind, creating the illusion of pain or pleasure. This illusion will keep us away from the ultimate Truth. Truth desires nothing. When there is no ego preference, all is equal and content with trust and freedom. This transforms the emptiness into Oneness.

My ego gave me the illusion of pain. I have been doing the Journey process[7] on forgiveness.

---

[7] *The Journey* by Brandon Bays gives powerful introspective meditations for both physical and emotional issues. The author healed herself from a stomach tumour. I am a journey practitioner. For seminars see infoeurope@thejourney.com.

13 January. Day Thirteen

My attachment to the five body senses has been diminishing during the past few days. I realised my taste for food had changed. I could have a cold piece of bread; in that I found my contentment. There did not seem to be a preference anymore.

I realised that both the fragrance of the flowers, in their purity, and the smell of the shit that I had previously trodden in, were in fact just smells. The shit was the recycled food that had nourished the body of an animal. There was a truth that took away the yucky feeling I would have had before. I realised my self-righteous ignorance was being seen and freed.

My need for human touch was diminishing; I knew the reality of the Truth. When my coat was dry and warm or cold and drenched—it just was. There was no preference; it was just an observation. My cold, frozen shoes were warmed by my feet as I walked. There was a trusting that happened naturally. Days passed and preference for soft, warm clothing faded. I gave many clothes away.

One night I observed my body was slightly cold yet there was contentment and peace within. Only later in the night did I realise there was no heating in the house. In bed cold came and cold went. My husband worked during the night, but I had no fear though I was on my own until the morning. My son came home late. It was his journey. He did not represent me. All my labels—wife, mother, teacher, and so forth—began to shed like layers of uniforms, falling away from me. The pure divine that permeated through all my labels was the same divine energy that was moving in my son, guiding us both perfectly on our journeys. My previous disgust of the smell of booze and disgust for the mess in his room diminished. Just in this moment my son had gone out, enjoyed himself, and here he was now sleeping, waking, and moving.

I felt whatever I saw was beautiful. The 'I am' meditation taught me all that I saw was a part of me. I was a part of it all, whether it was a tree, leaf, shit, grass, slippery mud, or water. I was a part of it all, even the rocks and the stones. Everything was a part of me. As days passed, I felt the totality of being inside and outside the concept of form. As a bird I felt my body swaying in flight; as the lake I felt the waters floating around me; I felt I was the sounds, the very friction of movement between the tyres of the car on the road; I felt one with the pressure of the vehicles on me (the road). When I felt I was the light, I felt the same ray in everything. I felt the same love for the rubbish, empty alcohol bottles, and beer tins thrown in my garden. I picked them up and placed them in the bin. I observed I was not touched by anything. There were no words in my mind; all I felt was peace in my body. I felt no preference, whether good or bad, for whatever I saw. I used to love the countryside, the beautiful scenery; now the greyness became as valuable as a sunlit day. A deep gratitude and love blossomed from within. The conscious meditation ceased. Life **became** the meditation.

Within the birdsong, dogs barking, wind rustling, children playing, and cars speeding, I heard nothing but silent peace within. Children at school swore and in discussing their use of language they replied that all they had heard was swearing at home for fifteen years of their lives and how could they suddenly change? I asked them to speak with conscious care and they did. When they looked at me, I could see their deep love; underneath the words the same light was flourishing. In the core of every sound is silence. In that silence is the vibration of Truth. God in Truth is the vibration of love.

I listened less to music, even prayer songs. I could hear the silence dancing, sweeping, relaxing, and trusting through me. The music within had reduced my desire for manufactured music.

Learning:

I realised that by trusting in the Lord's grace, we know that he is always there to hold our hands and protect us. Sometimes this may be through the mediation of another.

The moon played hide and seek—a metaphor for our glimpses of God's light. When we forget our God connection, we believe that we are alone. When we go within ourselves, our God light always shines.

The sun continuously emits God's love and light; even in the darkness of night it is reflected by the moon to guide us. When we walk in our own shadow, we become limited, whilst when we walk in the light, we experience boundlessness and freedom. When in shadow, we can focus towards the light, which burns through the illusions and negative beliefs that we use to limit ourselves.

Living in the conscious mind and in a time-pressured society—within the treadmill of routine—we forget to listen to the wisdom of the unconscious mind that is always awake. When we listen to the voice of ego, we separate ourselves from purifying our lives and from the presence of God within us. We are called to be like the birds, responding to each day dawning, inviting us to come home in each moment to God's light and love within ourselves. In light there is no darkness, and the miracle is that the darkness transforms into light. The ego and God cannot exist in one mind. When in ego, the pure infinite mind is absent. It is only the pure infinite mind that can take you to God consciousness.

When the lake is silent, there is stillness and peace; its surface is mirrorlike, reflecting all of the life that surrounds it.

Our interpretations are the projections of our thoughts, beliefs, and prejudices. These thoughts become projected into the body and onto the screen of life's story. We react to images we hold on to from the past, blaming others and unable to forgive. This story acts itself out again and again until we take ownership of our limited thoughts and wake up to the Truth.

In anger the waters of our body splash, crash, and shake with desires—if only I could have this or that. The waters create flooding; we project and vomit our feelings onto others, drowning and suffocating them. Like the sounds on the surface of the vessel of our body, we become loud; our thoughts become loud, our actions become loud. We lose sight of the peace of the lake within; we want only what is outside. As we overspend, our wants become greater, and we become miserable, seeking one desire after another to comfort ourselves with things. We look past the lake into a distorted mirror that is the denial of our true abundant and peaceful selves.

When the lake is still, there is silence; in that silence there is peace. In that peace there is Truth. The true overall picture is seen with understanding and clarity. We realise the water of our very being is never limited to just the vessel we are in—our body, our landscape. We experience and see the same water that makes up the lake or makes up ourselves and everything that we see. The same droplets of water are in the clouds above the lake, in the rain, the dewdrop on the grass, in the roots, on the leaves, the trees, in the ducks paddling on the lake, and the aquatic life in the water below. Everything is made up of the same water.

I experience I am not limited to the size or shape of my body vessel. I am in everything. I begin to love everything around me as I see these droplets of water that compose all of our bodies.

In the same way, when humans see the love, light, and God realisation within, we see the Truth of God's love and purity, which binds everything and everyone. In this there is forgiveness, acceptance, and contentment. Everything we see is a reflection of our love, God's love. Lies and illusions fade away, only Truth prevails. We see the love, light, and Truth within all. The God in me and the God in all is revealed.

The pull of energy diminishes when the five sensory doors let everything pass through with equal joy. The pure love energy cannot be drained by the illusions of desires and preferences. As the five slaves (senses) of the mind close the doors of illusion, the expansion of the consciousness of light, love, forgiveness, and freedom becomes boundless and penetrates through into the aura and infinity. The lake no longer has to destroy the body of its vessel to leak and flood what is beyond its holding space. In raising its awareness in consciousness, it begins to realise its being, its water, is everywhere. It is freedom in space. It is the universe itself.

As this month's prayer[8] conveys, when you conquer the mind, it bows, becoming one with the soul; the soul unites us with the very core of the Creator that is within us and we become part of the whole universe and existence.

14 January. Day Fourteen

My husband and I woke up late due to his night shift. At the lake there was a diversity of birds. The swan family came with its brown cygnets to eat the bread. I realised how the birds protected their young; the swan mother pecked at her cygnets and safety was paramount. When one duck took a piece of bread, flocks of birds came to snatch it. I realised when one bird is greedy, it affects the whole flock; likewise, when one member of kin goes astray in greed, the energy of the family boat is rocked.

If people did not feed their desire for greed, they would be content with what they have. When people go beyond their means and lie, in fact they withhold themselves from the very essence of their own beautiful soul.

I have a calling for surrender, yet there is a resistance in my body. As I observe my busy mind and feelings, anger and confusion are draining me. I want to let go of judgement and grow from this situation. Could I have provided a kinder environment earlier? Could I have created space for them to speak their truth? Had I avoided them in my unconscious fear and ignorance, preventing them from speaking their truth just in case I had to give up my free-dom and support them financially? As my ego asked question after question, I observed, there was a 'them' and 'me'. In that separation how could we ever meet and the story end?

Knowing God is all forgiving and in his abundance we are blessed, I felt the gift is to surrender to him totally in full gratitude and feel blessed for everything I have.

Learning

It is amazing how in Oneness there is vitality, vastness, and zest for life in Truth. Yet in the mind there is a cage; there is the lie of separation, aloneness, pain in illusions. Once coming out of the mind trap, it is a relief, an embracing, wide-open, all-accepting homecoming that sets us free. We can just be the empty space through which all life, all projections are just dancing and vibrating.

15 January. Day Fifteen

It was a mild morning at the lake, and I saw a soft, bright, large light in the grey sky. It came gently and disappeared back into the clouds. I learnt that the Lord shows his miracles to his pilgrims in remarkable ways. I wanted to nudge my husband so that he could share this moment, but listening to and trusting my inner guidance, I knew this moment was sacred, just for me.

I learnt that the sound of water greeting the bank was like a gentle prayer. When the mind is quiet, the few thoughts that come will not engage with the mind; they just drift, joining the prayer with their positive vibrations of Truth. When my mind was busy and noisy, I could not hear the beauty of the natural sounds.

I could feel the molecules of this boulder break as it cleared through my system, leaving me feeling light. This weightlessness, like speckles in the shaft of light, was spreading out from within me, until I became the spaces in between. I realised this weightlessness is only felt when one becomes true to Truth, which cannot be contained as it changes in every moment, revealing itself in new ways.

I understood that when I work in my Truth, out of love from the bottom of my heart, the other person can only interpret my Truth through the filter of their own experience and belief systems. I have to be open, to accept where they are at that moment in time.

Light cannot pass through any solid mass, it is only when the mass disintegrates that the light can permeate into the spaces, and with the continuing breakdown of the particles, the light becomes all. I realised that the illusion of pain is created by density breaking down. Enlightenment for me is when I truthfully feel the emotion and am not touched by it. Opening up into this space of Oneness, freedom, and weightlessness, which is made up of stillness, I am free to penetrate through the space of everything. The illusion of pain is the molecular breakdown and I am the space that embraces it. This free-flowing light within the spaces of all molecules is the eternal state of pure, untouchable Truth.

These forty days of pilgrimage are not over by any means, yet the learning is magnificent—to honour everything and to honour our Truth. Finally Truth is being spoken. I feel so humbled, so open in surrender to all that is yet to come.

Learning:

If we are not truthful to ourselves deep within, how can we be truthful to others? If we cannot hear others and only want to hear what makes us feel good, then how can that be the ultimate Truth, the Truth of the whole? It is only through hearing can we learn to grow, reflect, love, polish, change, and evolve.

16 January. Day Sixteen

It was mild and raining this morning. Silent ripples played on the surface of the still lake. In serene peace my thoughtless mind was without its ego-commentator. Contentment and the lake embraced me, contrasting against the noise and bustle of the busy road, like the difference between the awakened and sleeping mind.

The road represents the modern, mechanical, noisy, and chaotic time and age. This automatic rushing is all performed in the absence of mind wakefulness. The formless lake represents the permanent Truth that is unchanging, bowing only to nature's seasonal time. I realised without experiencing the lake, the rushing energy of the road would drain me. Without this comparison I would be stuck in the density and illusion of the material realm.

Walking through the slippery mud, I prayed and knew the Lord would save me.

I found a lump under my left breast which seemed very hard, firm, and big. My friend did the physical Journey on me, establishing my secondary gain. Going into my past, my younger self told me that when I had my youngest son, the only time I could be with my children or do my writing was when I was ill in bed. This prevented my younger self from living in her Truth and being strong enough to stand up for herself. It shut her down to life, fun, and laughter; it prevented her from playing with her children or going out. This old belief had not served her. This old belief was that I needed to be ill to justify having time to do what I wanted to do. After the Journey process, it was replaced with a new, healthy, empowering belief: **I am strong and healthy and will go through all life's experiences with trust and deep love, gratitude, and reverence, knowing the Lord is always there for me and my family.**

The red dusk had put the world to sleep and dream; now the dawn was awakening, heralding the new day. A veil lifted from my eyes to receive this precious gift from the

Guru; the birth of the new day was like the birth of a newly born child of golden light coming from the womb of God's love. Each birth of a new day is the innocent, pure miracle of the Divine's expression.

A celebration is taking place next door; their first child has been born and is coming home. My sister and a teacher at school will be having their babies soon. It is a sacred year.

I went to the doctor today and had my lump examined. I know that my miracle body is healing itself; old, stored negative beliefs, blocks, victimhood, and self-abuse are leaving me to replace the cells with health, peace, and joy.

If this gift of day is my last, I will praise the Lord with gratitude for this sacred time I have received. I thank the Lord for my beautiful family, relatives, and friends. I thank the Lord for these valuable breaths I have shared with all I have known in this world.

17 January. Day Seventeen

This ego can be wild at times. I howled like a dog, pushing everyone away, my mouth wide-open and screaming for help. I wanted to support this person, yet more loans were against my so-called belief system.

What a fool I was, to hold such a belief!! I had grieved over all these lies, yet I am the one who sheds her lies continuously. Is it really true that I do not like loans??

In a spark of Oneness, the Self revealed itself and I melted, realising that everything was on loan—my body, my spine, my breath, my life, family, banks. Everything was on loan.

Everything.

Nothing I held was true; as soon as I held onto any word or belief, it melted, for there was a deeper Truth that somehow dissolved everything I ever knew to be true at all. I lay in dancing emptiness until I became one in its vibration.

18 January. Day Eighteen

The strong wind caused the waves to soak us, as they rushed up from within the gaps in the wood. Their violent, miniature mountains grew and descended to be destroyed at the bank, one after another. I realised that we are all born to die, the cycle repeating itself until we liberate ourselves with the true realisation of freeing karma. This very pause between the mountain of waves rising and falling contained the formula of peace, boundless trust, and love.

I had cried so much last night that today I could not get up. Whilst listening to the prayers, my body felt heavy and floppy, and without energy. I curled up into foetal position (the baby pose in yoga). My forehead lay on the floor, bowing, begging for help. I nearly nodded off to sleep. At school tiredness contained me. The pupils seemed so angry; one child broke a photo frame, and glass shattered everywhere. At one point I felt myself collapse and my eyes flood with tears. I held them back until I went into the staff room where the tears just poured. I felt I could not handle this heavy pain inside my body or see the violence outside. It was not aimed at me but everyone. Yet amongst it all, I realised this was a test showing how tolerant and strong some children were. They had taken so much abuse in their young lives, and yet they had the strength to usually hold it together. It is at times like this golden saints are chosen; God's workers are blessed and rewarded. Without adversity, what would be the barometer? This storm, this energy comes to be balanced; how could I eliminate and decrease this karma, which somewhere during my soul's journey I had created? With positive, detached reaction and with gratitude for this karma's final release, I could harness my path to the Truth—a path of total harmony, bliss, peace, and abundance.

Learning:

I realised how belief systems not challenged and a mind not questioned could drain a person of their life-force energy. The unhealthy emotions were our teachers, reminding us our thinking needed to be cleansed to reveal the Truth.

I learnt how folk might feel, in their darkness, confusion, and weight causing them to drink themselves blindly into debt. I realised how gambling and share loss was a redistribution of money from someone who had previously lost it. It was recycled energy.

I realised this financial issue was our teacher. It could be from a previous incarnation. Debt is karma. I know I will gain a deep, permanent understanding from this issue. I rest in surrender.

My friend paraphrased from the bible, saying, '**Instead of criticising the dust in somebody else's eye, first take the beam out of your own.**' Before criticising another, it is important to sort yourself out. I remember a saying, '**When we give to others, we give to ourselves.**' We are one source, from which we come and to which we go. Thus forgiveness forgiving another means I give permission to forgive myself for the karma that I have produced in the projection onto the movie screen, which is my reality. I was the author and the projections are the reactions of my past life, playing themselves out for me to see, so I can shed, learn, and evolve. The world is always so kind to me; all it wants is the 'I' to die in this existence. It wants me to wake up and stay awake in Truth, where all suffering transforms into serenity.

19 January. Day Nineteen

The lake water was high from previous rain and fierce wind. The ducks on the lake put their beaks in the water, searching for food. I realised we, as humans, keep our heads submerged, searching for food and material possessions in our endless greed.

I prayed for my whole family. I prayed my sons would be holy, healthy, and happy. I prayed we could all learn to forgive fully, to heal ourselves and learn to trust and love deeply.

Learning:

Be like the lotus; although its roots are in filth, as the mind is in its illusion of *maya* (a Hindu term for the illusory nature of the world), its head looks above, at the sun. Looking at the sun, there is no shadow or illusion. Be like the lotus. Are we looking at forms, objects, Truth, attachment, or freedom? There is a path to God when we are living in our highest infinite Truth.

Harjinder Kaur Chohan

20 January. Day Twenty

The lake was serene at 4.00 a.m. this morning. The sky was dark, yet soothing light glistened on the waves. The deepest tranquillity I have ever felt arose within me, opening the petals of my heart. The very core of me felt loved by the caressing, gentle fingers of Mother Nature, cradling her child deep in this pure, holy morning (Amrit Vela). I realised how Mother Nature embraces her child with so much love, how I can feel her delicate, gentle hands in the deepest corpuscles of my being. I felt her love was washing me clean, and she was awakening the light within, deep in my core. Walking back I realised my hands were in prayer pose. I felt so humbled, grateful, and open to everything I met on the way home. The light and love of Mother Nature was in all.

I learnt this holy morning hour of prayer that there were no words that could describe this time. I felt such a deep, enveloping love. Mother Nature seems so pleased that I shared this special time with her, before dawn. The Mother waited to caress her awakened children deeply in her warmth before the rest of the world awakened with its ego crying to be heard and fed. Only a few people are awake at this time, so Mother Nature hears us whilst the rest of the world is asleep. I could feel the vibrations of her consciousness and became one with the waves, the trees, water, and grass. It was so easy to become one; whilst my ego mind was asleep, God consciousness in me stayed awake.

I took my husband to Kundalini Tantric yoga,[9] praying it would help us clear our karma. My husband and I sat opposite each other, as we held a posture for sixty-two minutes. We looked into each other's eyes. I saw God in his eyes. I just could not stop laughing.

21 January. Day Twenty-one

I was awakened from a dream in which a deceased relative held my children (who were younger) in a van; she also said she would kill me. A saint came and saved us. I did reiki,[10] and using the symbols, went back in to understand the meaning of this dream. I was told I should not under-estimate another's intention. I can only know my own

---

[9] Yogi Bhajan says, 'The beauty of White Tantric Yoga is that it is subtle, it is exalting, and it works to give you the mastery of life. It helps to overcome the obstacles of the subconscious mind and grow in truth. Our minds release 1000 thoughts per wink of an eye. Some of these thoughts get lost in the uncon-scious and some get stuck in the subconscious and affect the conscious mind. These thoughts become feelings, emotions, desires, fantasies or multi-realities. Instead of mastering our mind, often our mind and thoughts rule us and this pressure can eat us up inside. White Tantric Yoga enables you to break through those subconscious blocks so that you can experience a happier and richer life. In the shortest time you can experi-ence release from much of the burden and extra weight you carry in your head.' Extracted from KYTA for January 2009

intention. If I see God in everyone, I can forgive them at a deep level. This helps me untie the painful cords attaching me to those people and allows me to move on. My only duty is to know my self. In this journey of Truth, the Lord will always protect me. Sometimes He will send His angels or saints down to save me.

During the meditation and prayers, Yogi Bhajan came and sat in my body. His hands held coloured prayer beads (*mala*) and he wore a maroon shawl with cream border embroidery. He allowed me to look out from my third eye and I saw a brilliant white light. I could see him as this eye was outside of me, observing my body. I asked him something. He looked directly into me. My being understood; I needed to be quiet.

Yogi ji told me a lot of things, some of which I remember. He told me I, as a yoga teacher, needed to work between the means of my karmic sheet (*chardar*) and not to look beyond my means. People should have only what they can pay off monthly, whilst living a balanced life. The pain of wasting money and using it negatively has a powerful energy pull. Young couples and teenagers need to be

[10] Reiki (pronounced Ray-key) is a Japanese word meaning universal life force energy; this energy is all around us. Reiki is a system of natural healing which evolved in Japan from the experience and dedication of Dr Mikao Usui (d. 1926). There is no belief system attached to Reiki. It is possible to heal at any level of being: physical, mental, emotional, or spiritual. I am a Reiki master. With this alternative medical treatment, healing energy is channelled from the practitioner to the patient to enhance energy and reduce pain, stress, and various ailments.

helped to value monetary exchange, and it is important to teach them to live in Truth, to know **simplicity is vital.** Only by seeing our Truth, can we learn to change things around us.

Before Yogi ji left, he gave me a veil that covered my head, face, and body. This veil melted into my skin, my bones, my organs, and blood. Entering my heart, it exploded into light. I became all light. He put prayer beads (*mala*) around my head, heart, and palms. These beads exploded, illuminating all of me. He said, this veil will consume all lies, the dirt (*mal*) of this life, and make everything pure and sparkling in the name of Truth. He gave me his blessings and put his hand on my head before he left.

At the lake the family of five swans came to be fed. I learnt we five as a family will be fine. In the past I had seen the glistening light and shadows on the waves look like little mountains; today they looked like the wings of swans getting ready to fly.

Learning:

The waves were similar to the emotions our body releases. When we stay still and detached and just observe the Truth, these emotions are given wings to fly into freedom. When we avoid our Truth and stuff the emotions down, mountains arise and explode on the surface of our body, causing resistance, anger, fear, pain, and disease (dis-ease).

It is said we communicate 3 percent verbally and 97

percent by body language. Where there is anger, war is created even before the exchange of words and energy is lost. By looking outside and thinking the other person is the one who gave us this emotion of anger, we fuel it and the war continues. Oneness is revealed only by recognizing that anger is just a wave that was created from the same water of the lake. In this undying existence from which we are all created and united we can begin to heal the wounds we created from the illusions of pain.

In receiving this immense life-force energy, the door of the mind opens into the present. Here, we are finally at home where mind cannot exist. There is no past, no future, just this moment. This experience allows us to see, with eyes of Truth, the expression of all creation in its golden glory. Every corpuscle in our being bows in gratitude and humility to this universal, loving, vibrant energy and we are rejuvenated and overwhelmed by the wow factor!

22 January. Day Twenty-two

The water was calm, gentle, and still. The bread and seeds floated on the lake. When I float on the surface of my emotions, I am affected by the highs and lows of the ride. As I sink into the pure water, I disintegrate, becoming one and whole. In this deep drowning, the Oneness of the ocean releases me into this vast, boundless freedom. There should be only one desire: freedom, or Oneness. In that we become everything and everyone, a united realm. Emotions and dramas cannot touch the ocean. The sharks, fishes, surfers, tsunamis cannot attack or imprison the ocean. The waves come, winds blow, sun evaporates, yet the ocean is unaffected. It remains free and unchanging in this Oneness.

Early this morning, the birds did not touch the bread; they are so content and have no selfish hunger. They respond to their senses and biological clock and move accordingly.

23 January. Day Twenty-three

In the meditation I experienced being 'God'. As a massive giant all was inside me; the planets were marbles and everything else, play dough. We were tiny specks, dark dots, or candles attracted to God's light. I realised when God inhaled, He absorbed the atmosphere we humans had created, and as he breathed out clean, radiant, and pure love, light and acceptance filled the air and our world.

The sky, an emerald blue with a green horizon, shone brightly. Stars sparkled upon the frost. The silver-sprayed platform, with its untouched whiteness, welcomed us. I realised when times seem hard, it is because we cannot see the bigger picture. God's hidden agenda is to our advantage in that moment. Likewise, the frozen mud had made it easier for us to walk upon the ground.

The lake shone and I realised we were all part of God's breath. This direct experience pierced me with razor-like, clear awareness. The same breath was in everything; in plastic, metal, and in the cygnets who, with the swans, came so close to us this morning. This awareness of God's breath being in everything blossomed in my heart, opening it as wide as the universe.

At school during the teacher's morning meeting, I experienced an enormous amount of love fill my whole body. It was as if I were a part of everyone's breath. Direct experience flowed inside me and every corpuscle in my being knew that God's loving breath is in all of us, everything and everyone. In this Truth we are all connected and whole.

With direct experience I connected to this breath of Oneness. In that breath, Gods love, warmth, light, and spirit set me ablaze in amazing awareness of overflowing love and gratitude. My whole body melted, connecting in love to all I met that day. I thanked the Lord for this immense, overflowing river of love, which unites all.

24 January. Day Twenty-four

During meditation I experienced a love beyond my physical existence. I carried out a simple Journey process in which I was able to forgive all those who had hurt me in the past. I forgave all those in hell (if there is one), in this world, and beyond. I forgave them for hurting me, knowingly and unknowingly. I opened my being to receive forgiveness from all my past beings when I had intentionally or unintentionally hurt others. From this I received abundant, pure love from a deep source of freedom. This left my blood, muscles, tissues, organs, bones, and skin emanating love back to their source. This love was felt from the very *pranic* energy of my being. Everything continued as normal around me, yet I was only aware of the love-God's breath—that gave life to all living things. In stillness, I could feel this pure silence. The vibration of *pranic* energy connected to its source, creating overflowing love. I fell in love with this air that filled all living things. I felt we were all part of one love—God's breath. In reverence and gratitude I bowed to this wisdom and experience that united us all as one.

Dog walkers and their pets had left their footprints in the snow. In our reaction to action, we create footsteps (karma) on our path. Karma can only be erased by the forgiveness of God's love. Freedom comes from total forgiveness and gratitude for the path we have left behind. It is this very path that has brought us to this perfect moment.

At the beautiful blue lake, the stars sparkled brightly above. The three loyal cygnets came and waited for their bread while we finished the prayers. We both saw a shooting star speedily arcing into the northeast.

Millions of tiny waves and big ripples filled the lake. I understood that when forces of negativity such as anger, jealousy, bitterness, and rejection appear, we reduce in size, becoming separate from the whole. Enlightenment is when we become part of the whole; when no colour, form, personality, behaviour, or language can separate us. We are connected by one breath. As I returned from this experience, mind, thoughts, and emotions came, yet the experience of one breath continued to connect me to all things, emanating pure love throughout me. With each breath and heartbeat, I could feel mountains of love move with the breath in my body, uniting with the breath of the universe. I felt so humbled, light, weightless, free, and expansive.

Driving the car to college, I felt as if I were motionless. The car was moving, yet I was in this energy field, moving from one space of myself to another. When we become a part of everything, we just move into ourselves again and again. As my dentist drilled through my tooth, his soft, warm hands were God's breath of love. His hands were an instrument of God's breath, my breath.

Learning:

At college I realised why I was closer to some students than others. When two spirits are set alight by God's

Truth, their consciousness meets in realisation of God's love breathing through us, of every moment being our second chance to realise this precious Truth. Our level of purification lifts our vibration, thus we connect deeper to those at the same level of vibration. God's breath of love is in all, yet depending on our conscious willingness, we enter this temple within. Once in the temple, we can see the Truth. As we cleanse and de-clutter, we become weightless. We penetrate through the physical body. In our willingness to surrender and purify, we allow God's breath within to meet God's breath outside. God's love expands, vibrating at a higher, faster frequency. The chakras, whirlwinds of God's love, circulate; everything inside the body moves. Molecular breakdown of dense energy occurs, uniting and purifying us into this Oneness. We are the light inside and the light outside.

The pinnacle of the triangle temple is the summit where God consciousness resides. Everything becomes one. This powerful peak is the highest, deepest, purest vibration of attainment. Once at that summit, all is equal and Truth comes from Oneness. God's energy of love will lead us to it as soon as we choose to enter the temple of our soul. The temple's divine purpose is to know Truth in God's love. Our destination and freedom are in God's love. Yet at this point in my life, to experience that I was related to each person through God's breath was a revelation.

Harjinder Kaur Chohan

25 January. Day Twenty-five

The gorgeous blue sky was brightly starlit and the earth glittered with frost, enabling me to appreciate the birth of this new day. The sun was born, the sky blazing with its red, celebrating dawn, each plant bowing and growing towards the light. How could we stay sleeping; how could we postpone living this life in love and gratitude and own this magnificent beauty? How could we take it all for granted and be unaware everything is a gift on loan? I feel so privileged to be a part of this day.

I carried out a four-cornered meditation on forgiveness. I forgave the past, healing my ancestors, and I forgave the past lives, present, and future that separated me from my Truth. Forgiveness is the key to unlocking the chains which tie us to our past, robbing us from our present moment.

Learning:

On the journey back from school, the horizon was a magnificent orange red. The sun was rising in a different part of the world, leaving in its celebration a red ember. We are nurtured in this balance of darkness and light. The earth and our biological clock are magnificent creations. The forces which rotate this world and hold it together dazzle me and I feel deep humility in response to the magic and miracle we are living in. Why should I react to karma with uncertainty when such a great force is taking care of us? I need to laugh, sit, and enjoy the game of life the Lord is playing. Like the karma of my creation, this world and its interactions are the Lord's making. If I am willing to surrender and trust this force that takes care of universes, I should effortlessly enjoy this life with awe and reverence for all the miracles that take place. The Lord is responsible for all of creation and I need to rejoice in this miracle that I am only responsible for me.

My ophthalmologist friend loves working with the eyes because, as she says, behind the eye there is a beautiful sunset; it is the window to our soul. Yet we can only see it through another's eye. My body shone in Truth. Sunsets are in me; planets are in me; the universe is in me. So magnificent and magical is this body that it is made in the image of this world and beyond. Once we feel nature within, we can see the Truth of its power outside.

26 January. Day Twenty-six

Two swans waited for us today. As they dipped the bread into the water to soak before swallowing it, I experienced a simple, yet deep truth; I understood the value of water. Without it we could not survive. We need it to swallow food and to transport nutrients and gases around the body in our blood. Everything is and needs water. With prayers it is water that becomes holy (*amrit*). We need to honour water. It is through water all the chemistry of life happens—in our bodies, on this Earth, and beyond.

I realised that the skeletal trees were untouched by the changing weather because they trusted in God's creation.

These past six years of my life I had become a fisherwoman, going inside my consciousness, throwing the net, catching the sharks and poisonous bodies, and removing them with my intention. I was then opening the oyster shells of memories which were holding me back, seeing their Truth, and releasing them into the consciousness of God's infinite love and light.

I felt so grateful for Brandon Bays' book 'The Journey' and Reiki, both of which had healed me so deeply, allowing me to go into the core issues and become in touch with my universal love energy. I felt so grateful to prayer, meditation, and Kundalini yoga that had directed me in a new light. I realised all these events were part of my deepest prayer to know my Self and to go on this journey within. This allowed me to clear my true home and empty out stuff that I did not need any more. In no way am I just the skeleton, yet I look forward to becoming the skeleton. I need to first open and see my self, exposed and vulnerable with my weaknesses and pains. I need to forgive myself and those whose pain I still hold. I need to trust the Lord and surrender to that trust. Only then will I be naked in humility; when my pains and mistakes are exposed to my self, all the emotional attachments, such as anger, rejection, grief, and hurt, will take leave. When I become the skeleton like the trees, I will become equal to all: tornadoes, frost, sunlight, rain, and all the weathers of my life. When I become nothing, ready to burn to ashes, the Lord's love and grace will cloak me in leaves-in true abundance. The same leaves will become the nutrients that feed and sustain me. When I totally shed, I will be ready to be cloaked anew.

27 January. Day Twenty-seven

Nothing written. Just silence.

28 January. Day Twenty-eight

The five swans were waiting for us this morning. I felt tension and niggling irritation from the hustle and bustle of the noisy commuters and the wind driving and rushing through the waves. I saw fear in the mother swan as she protected and pinched her cygnet's neck to pull it away. My husband interpreted this as her greed to eat the bread. I realised a simple truth; although we were seeing the same action, our perception was different due to the filters of experiences, beliefs, and emotional blocks within. When we have greed, then we will see greed. When we have fear, then we will see fear. When we have suspicion, then we will see trust abused.

Our ego personalities, which we have developed throughout our lifetime, will create a false truth to make us feel superior and powerful over others; we feel this through separation of self or segregation of certain groups. However, when we see from God's Truth, our being will see from a place of forgiveness and pure, unconditional love. From this place, we see through God's eyes the union of all creation.

In a place of worship (Gurdwara) where I sat, the prayer and sacred music broke all the illusions of my physical body into fragments. My skin melted, my body crumbled in this love, and my blood evaporated in this warmth. All that was left was a red dawn. Out of this came light and the waves of light joined the vibration outside me with the melody of purity and divinity. My boundless light illuminated, and love emanated out into everything. Then a sword split everything and I saw a silver oyster break open; from within the oyster, a silver ball appeared. The sword placed this weightless ball into my heart. A nameless feeling penetrated my being. Questions arose and fell away.

Learning:

I realised this awareness is boundless; everything comes and goes. Everything is the mirror of our self. Everything is a part of our being, our wholeness that is projected from within. The commentator in the mind, which wants to draw us away from this awareness, still speaks, yet the infinite Self is so open that there is nothing to control anymore. In this, all acceptance, love, and warmth give everything freedom to just be, and gently in that freedom everything becomes one with its true nature. Dramas, stories, past, and future dissolve because nothing inside wants to engage with it; this awareness welcomes all with love. In the ocean sharks swim, people play, boats sail, oil spills, cargoes get looted, yet the ocean is undisturbed. Planets move, stars explode, satellites orbit, yet the universe is unaffected. This infinite force knows exactly what it is doing. The universe, the air, the breath is moving us into freedom, into this Oneness, this formless, unlimited, eternal, sacred, serene stillness that is omnipresent.

29 January. Day Twenty nine

My exhausted body came alive as it saw the swan family awaiting us. It was like a *satsang* (meeting of lovers of Truth) waiting for its *prashad* (blessing). I felt so connected that I could feel the fruit blossom in my heart, which humbly opened and bowed to this joy and miracle.

My husband had made five breads this morning; it was as if five beloved saints had come to receive these sacred gifts and prayers. I experienced this divinity washing away my sins. A simple realisation awoke in me. We have five senses; we have five digits on our hands and feet. Our feet carried us to the lake. There are five members in our family. In one numerology I had heard five was the number of the teacher; here we were the five students and our five teachers were the swans. There were five rivers in the Punjab; Guru Gobind ji[11] created five Sikhs (*punj pyare*) in the Sikh Khalsa; there were five pandits in the Hindu war of the Mahabharata, 101 on one side and 5 on the other. There are five elements in the Chinese philosophy of Taoism: metal, wood, water, fire, and earth. In Japanese philosophy and in Neo-Paganism there are five similar elements. In Christianity the mystic Theresa of Avila spoke of how the five senses were shed before entering the inner castle. On my way back from work there were five blobs of bird droppings on my car windscreen, grouped together to form a pentagon. My mum always says bird droppings are a lucky sign. (Why? I do not know.) I am sure there are many other things signifying the importance of this number.

[11] Guru Gobind Singh was a prominent seventeenth century Guru of the Sikhs. Gobind is also one of the names of Krishna, the principal Hindu deity.

Learning:

Nothing happens by chance; everything is interlinked. Our journey in life is magic and just amazing. I felt so blessed to be on this pilgrimage. All the deep knowledge that I had acquired from religious and enlightened scriptures was opening into an experience beyond understanding. It felt as if, instead of reading the text, I was tasting it from deep within. It was as if the words were a living vibration of light and peace without a language. In the moment the scripture is read, there is a pause of absolute stillness and silence afterwards. Not a sound is spoken. This is the point where there is no observer anymore. In this place where the 'I' and all experiences dissolve, the Creator itself creates and tastes its own expression.

The swans seemed hungry and ate quickly. I realised we need to eat with gratitude and love and taste the food's blessing. We are in such a hurry to eat and possess things that we do not see the consequence of our actions or feel the joy in honouring everything in life as a gift. We battle, take, swallow, and hoard inside without looking at the gifts. Without reverence and gratitude, the gifts turn to rubbish and the goodness cannot be nourished. We squeeze away the juice and joy from life. Our eyes on the outside want to consume everything because we do not understand the gift is a reflection from the inside, bestowed upon us to cherish.

Harjinder Kaur Chohan

30 January. Day Thirty

In my meditation and prayers I carried out a Journey process on myself and realised I was healing, purifying, and enlightening all of my family and future family members. My chest felt heavy and my body exhausted, as if so much clearing was taking place within me.

At the lake the three cygnets waited with two coots. One coot took the bread, departing from its companion. I had watched the two coots share the corner of a bush in the lake for so long and they were usually together, yet today this one piece of bread separated them. A mallard chased another duck away. When I realised that duck had lost hope, I threw my last piece of bread towards it. As I was watching, I realised deeply that the Lord is always watching too. When we surrender fully to the Lord, in that moment we receive enlightened awareness and the true gifts of life.

Yesterday's bread was hard; I watched the swans wait until it softened before they ate it. I could hear their beaks dabbling in the water. Intently watching this, I realised this lake supports them totally. It is their home.

At school my head teacher talked to the children about tools. She said our words were important tools and we needed to learn ways of using them wisely. She spoke of how these tools helped us build relationships, harness our thoughts, and create our visions.

Returning from the lake, I realised the virtue of silence. There was no need to waste my breath or my words with those who did not listen to life or those who were not in a place to take responsibility for their actions. I realised I was hurting because someone had never heard me.

They had never heard me. I felt the silence of this truth.

I realised the truth in our breath is worth so much; if this truth is aligned with God's Truth, then we must save it for the company of saints or those who wish to listen. I realised how I hurt myself with my own created lies. Had I always heard others? Of course not. Can we always do that? Definitely not, especially since we are in our minds most of the time.

The truth was I had not always heard the gentle calling of my self. When in my thoughts, Truth gave me dramas in my life to wake me up. However, in trying to impress my personality and feed my thoughts, I got lost in my story and became hooked, drained, and seeking to be liked by others. I had not fully realised I could never love another or be loved. Two minds do not know what love is. Finally glimpsing the Truth—**I had not heard me**—I realised how lucky I was to find me, to have glimpses of walking into this Oneness. Like a cord, my Self was pulling me into its Self, each time the experience lasting longer, full of more energy, love, light, and joy. My Self wanted to share from this place of Oneness in order to reach others so that they may become collective universal energy of pure love and peace.

Learning:

We are so fortunate we have earth as our home. Yet are we satisfied? We have hands and feet, yet we cannot live in nature or trust it like the birds do. We limit ourselves; we cannot surrender everything to this environment, our home; nor can we trust this is all that we need. It is in the simple life with nature that we obtain happiness, peace, and pure abundance. Instead of this simple life, I have a heated home, hot and cold water from a tap, gas fire from a switch, light, warmth, material goods, and the world at my feet through the internet, TV, and telephone. We want everything at our doorstep, swimming pools, gardens, holidays, and cars and we do not want to walk. Yet we could be on holiday every day if we lived and breathed in nature. In appreciating nature, growing our own food, swimming in the lake (which my ancestors did), walking to work, playing on land, and feeling the wind, we could feel the embrace of the elements. Instead we create brick walls, block out living nature, and block the view from windows. We cannot see the sky, feel the breeze, hear the running streams or the birds. From one block building, we drive to another. Separated from our greater self, we feel empty. We create our own prisons and die to be free from them. Birds surrender, trust nature, and live in God's unconditional love.

31 January. Day Thirty-one

It felt as if the prayers had been deeply heard. As I scanned my body (*vipassana* meditation), my awareness became boundless, brilliant, white, loving light. I could feel a mass of molecules breaking in the centre of my body. The soothing prayers said, 'God is near and far'. This penetrated deep. There is no distance in God's love; he is a part of us, and it is only when ego enters, wanting recognition, name, and glory, that separation occurs.

In wonder, as I stepped through the front door, my husband pointed to our right. The sun was brilliant, blazing orange and red light with strips of cloud intersecting it. I suddenly realised, as my husband already had, that this in fact was the moon. I rushed to get the camera and take a picture, yet in the need to show others, I had lost the beauty of that moment. I had to be awake to feel its beauty; it could not just be seen. I stayed and watched as my body filled with warmth.

While walking, singing, chanting the prayers, and taking photos of the brilliant red skies, my camera batteries ran out at the moment I wanted to capture something fresh and new. In that moment, I realised there was nothing I could take; it was an experience of wonder at its best that could not be captured. The colours were so meaningful; the blue of the sky was healing us all. No wallpaper, paint, or picture could ever replace the colours of nature in each moment. The Lord is the artist. I need to just enjoy the colours of the ever-changing moment.

The daffodils, tulips, and exotic flowers were welcoming us; the glow of the moon embraced me with its love. I was as if in a different world. Despite the frost, I felt so warm and complete, filled with so much love that there was nothing else I needed.

This January prayer had become a part of my blood, yet tomorrow we would start a new set of prayers. I realised this prayer had cleansed layers of lies, illusions, and insecurities from within me. The major debts had been all sorted in two separate affordable monthly payments. I felt the arms of God within and around me. The temple, the holy sacred place within my heart, was transporting light, love, and freedom into my cells. We had been cleared of some big karma. I felt so joyous, so grateful for the gift of this new day.

Learning:

It was the last day of this prayer, and this gem, this gift was so powerful to behold. As one becomes One (Gobind), we see our sole purpose of life and existence. The function of this vehicle, our body, is to transport us to this enlightenment already within. In our darkest hour when we ask for help from our Lord, the sun reflects its light towards the moon of that night. With faith and trust we too will be transformed into this glory of our being. As the lotus looks up at the sun, we must look up to be saved, not below at our shadow or roots. The sky is a mirage of colours, yet both dawn and death of day is celebrated by different shades of red. I can feel this deep celebration that the red colour brings in its day. Nothing dies; it is always a birth of something new, awakened afresh, a new breath on a new stage. In our journey, at every moment, we are always at the beginning, yet our ego brings up the mess from the graveyards of our past and wishes to carry this burden from yesterday with us into this new day. If we could be like Mother Earth, who opens the curtains in such glory, we could truly honour this life.

1 February. Day Thirty-two

We have entered the door into a new universe. The lake water is so peaceful; tiny silver seed currents are flowing gently; the swans are sitting in silence. Nothing seems to move; in this stillness is the pearl of peace. This serene tranquil atmosphere is penetrating through our porous physical body. Eyes closed or open, in company or seclusion, our molecular mortal being breaks into dust, becoming a vast world of Gobind. In this I feel the peace of everything beyond words and knowledge, just an experience of being.

Harjinder Kaur Chohan

Learning:

It feels as if, from the main door, we have opened into the temple of Gobind. All is different: the birds, their song, the daylight. I get lost reading maps; how do the birds know their path in the air currents? Even through adversities, with their inner guidance, they trust the breeze. God has given them their inner compass, whereas we have lost ours due to focusing on the outside.

2 February. Day Thirty-three

The red sky was divided by greyness. I realised empty space was capturing the illuminating rays from the sun. As I chanted the prayer, my being opened and I realised a simple truth; every time that I had made a judgement of another, I had lied to my self. I had also in the past judged myself, and people might have said negative things to me once in a while and I had procrastinated and believed their lies. I had made excuses to stay small and invisible, dividing the skyline of my mind so my light could not shine in God's Truth. This peace was ambivalent to my conditioned mind. All space was taken up with lies and mind wars. This created action, thereby creating new karma.

I now felt as if I were at the beginning again.

I thought I was a truthful person, yet I was a liar. My judgements were lies. Now I gave myself the opportunity to release them by forgiving and giving myself permission to let go. How could anyone ever hate one person without hating everyone that had their DNA? This was a simple but a deep lie that revealed itself to me. In the core of everyone's being, they are an untarnished, pure being of Truth. It is only behaviour that one could find fault with, even though this behaviour is often simply a reflection of our own thoughts and misunderstandings. As a deep experience, I watched my lies break away from the painful necklace. I realised my thinking and words had to change if I was going to be truthful to Truth itself. Of course I would be in pain if lies were flowing into my thoughts; the resistance in the lie would be felt within the physical and emotional body, allowing me to be the core, manifesting agent of that person's behaviour.

Driving home from school, as if only the present moment had ever existed, I was awed by the scorching, massive, orange red sun in the blue sky. I felt flabbergasted in gratitude at the sun, which appeared to be a controlled sphere of a burning fire. Its flames of warmth, love, and light amazed me with how much the Lord was in control of everything. Then gratitude for water, breeze, and weather poured into me; I felt how deeply our well-being is nurtured. Just like the different types of weather, our emotions help us to grow and evolve, to move us through life and motivate and change our direction. As long as we do not become the emotion, but let it ride through us to its freedom, accepting all emotions equally, the emotion will leave in its space a gift of great learning.

As I returned from shopping, it was darkening. The sky had turned from blue and red to darkness. As I reversed my car, the moment captured me in deep reverence; I turned to see a large ball of silver shining brightly. The moon seemed bigger than I had ever noticed before. It pulled me into itself, welcoming me into its beauty. I felt so lucky. I had seen the sun, the moon, and the changes of colour in the sky. I bowed to grace. If God could control all the comings and goings of the sun, moon, sky, and watch over us, who was I to want to control anything in life, or have the notion that I ever did? I felt I wanted to just sit back, welcome with open arms whatever came my way, and enjoy the film that was being played out for me. I realised I am just the observer sitting in the cinema watching the screen of life.

3 February. Day Thirty-four

What magnificence! What indescribable glory! I bow in thankfulness to you Lord for this mere mortal to be a part of such wonder.

This morning, after the prayers of peace, I forgave others for an hour. I felt my chest muscles open. When I left home for our walk, I saw the bold, shining, full moon. I bowed to its glory. I had seen it last night before I entered our home and now before I entered nature's world. With such privilege, I chanted the prayers. I heard my being chant the prayers of last month intertwined with the prayers of this month. On our path to the lake, as if by a miracle, we stopped in amazement. The blazing, red, bold sun was on our left and the calm, solemn, full moon opposite, on our right. I whispered to my husband for us to both stand there in the centre, between them, receiving their energy. I stood there as if the next moment would not come. I laughed as I realised I had thought if we moved on, we would not be in the centre of this beauty, yet as we moved, this beauty followed us. In this revelation I experienced I was not moving; I was just entering the same space of God's breath. I realised I had never moved. Movement was an illusion. 'I' was the unlimited presence.

How lucky was I to see both lovers opposite each other and for my husband and me to share this glory. At the lake, the platform of wood on which we usually sat was replaced by fishermen rods. A photographer was taking pictures of the fragile frost skin floating on the shimmering lake. Its mist, full moon, and the swans and ducks together formed a picturesque scene, as if from paradise.

The swans stayed far away from the platform we usually sat on, which was now replaced by the rods. I managed to throw the bread far enough for them to eat. I realised the five swans had trusted us enough to come to us to be fed. Content, away from the rods they stayed. Some humans fight in greed; in their wanting they cannot see the nets and traps in life. Although intuitively trusting, the birds are aware of their own safety. They do not become slaves of their mind. Greed blinds and traps humans and then we complain. Birds are the angels of God teaching us so much.

The morning embraced me with its magic charm. Walking down the lane, the countryside was flooded with birds dancing, dogs running, and cows grazing. In the distance the lake scintillated through the gaps in the hedge. I was told by a friend the silver metallic moon was yin, female energy, also linked to the unconscious. Its sacredness was shown by the links to the cyclic rhythms of life and to the feminine monthly cycle controlling human fertility. The changing phases were connected to death and rebirth. The patience in the way the moon becomes whole enchants me. Just before the full moon I feel so emotional that I want to chant God's prayer over and over again.

The sun represents gold, yang, and male energy. I feel it represents the centre of our creative life energy, guiding our flow of direction and illuminating the path. It is what reminds me of the soul. It is what gives light to the darkness by illuminating the moon and stars and is always there for us, giving us vitality.

It has felt like walking across a bridge, with the energies

from the sun and moon giving us their love, strength, and power. We had woken up late today. Now I experienced there was no such thing as time; every moment was divine, everything moved in perfection. We were meant to walk into this alignment of the planets. We had been kept in our 'resting rooms' whilst the moments had called us into their perfection. I felt a freeing of old, stuck energy. I felt so blessed and grateful for this extraordinarily fulfilling morning.

The first jewel was the shooting star, then the red moon, then the alignment in our embrace between the sun and moon energies. I had experienced three jewels in two months and ten months left remained. I felt so lucky.

Learning:

Senseless mind talk takes us away from our internal processing and allows us to avoid facing, feeling, and learning from our own issues. I realised how important silence is to support the stillness of thoughtlessness and to receive the reward of peace, healing, and freedom.

The prayer revealed itself to me today. I thought I was the one running around, but in fact, it's all so simple. We are all still; the sun and moon appear to be moving. The mind gives the illusion we are moving. Movement of me walking disappeared. There was nowhere for me to go, to run to or from—no rushing, sprinting, or turning. I was stepping from one breath of stillness to another. God's breath was one.

4 February. Day Thirty-five

After prayer, meditation, yoga, or any inward process uniting soul, mind, and body, I realised, as yesterday, how important sacred silence is. It allows us to feel the raw pain of our past issues and receive the gift of release.

During this morning I processed and realised there was a big block of 'stuckness' inside me ready to move out. My husband and I both walked to the lake silently. In the frost the sky was bright red. The greeting moon was full. I felt protected by its presence, and as I looked up, I saw a red sketch of an enlightened being. It touched a chord within and I felt as if I would rise after this block was free. I just needed to believe in God fully and let go of the blame game.

The swans were standing in a line facing us near the far bank. Two coots charged across the water towards us but did not eat the bread. Maybe they were worried about yesterday's fishing rods and were cautious. The swans approached slowly. The parents pulled at the cygnets' feathers to stay away from the platform. They took the bread from the water but not from the platform. I realised they were still wary from yesterday.

Learning:

In order to forgive fully, I need to trust. Maybe the lesson for me was to trust myself. I asked myself the question, 'In what ways in my life had I not trusted myself?' I realised I did not trust myself fully in my healing work. If I had so much to deal with and remove in myself, how could I be a beacon to others? If this was so, then I was not fully trusting in God. My lesson was to identify all the ways I was not trusting God. Trust should be the foundation of our home. Trust must be established before forgiveness can take place fully.

5 February. Day Thirty-six

The waning moon shone brightly across the grey day. I felt a deep connection with the moon and sun, as if they were the parents who protected us wherever we were on this earth.

At the frosty, cold lake, two coots came towards the bread, and although it was right beneath their eyes, missed seeing it. Sometimes, like the coots, we are so close to our gift from God that in our hurry and anxiety our cluttered mind cannot see the treasure lying in front of us. From the mist of darkness, the swans slowly made their journey towards us before eating the bread. I realised that in searching for the swans, my heart had contracted. Perhaps a part of me had missed them. I experienced how one could get attached to giving. This attachment, in the long run, could cause disease and illness. When we give with expectation, it becomes our own nightmare.

Learning:

I experienced the unconditional love which God gives. I realised we must give openly, freely, fully unattached. Who knows whom the food is created for or who will taste it? I remembered that when we give, we are only giving to ourselves. It is all one flow of energy. It comes from and goes back to one source—God.

6 February. Day Thirty-seven

As I opened the front door, the moon shone brightly. At the lake, the bread slid further across the frozen crinkled waves, which had solidified like a silken ice fabric. The moon opposite our sitting place shone dim light onto the lake. No birds were near, yet in the distance the five swans had begun to travel in a line around the frozen part of the open water's edge. I felt their love ebbing in my pulse. Their fragile bodies trod gently on the ice towards us. Touching the ice, I felt its hard, sharp glassiness nearly cut me.

I realised two worlds were separated by this armour, the

lake and my being. I had worn armour to cover my authentic, Higher Self. Unlike before, the light of the moon could not swim, dance, glow, and disperse in the particles of the lake water. The frozen wrinkles and the dim light prevented us from seeing the true reflection.

When I travelled home from work, I saw the blazing sun cloud over. Its fire was so hot, yet so soft and pure. Its gentle embrace held me. My being recognised the joy our star, the shining sun, gives us. I understood how other planets have many suns and moons. I experienced the immensity of the infinite universe and this tiny me, which the ego thinks is all so important. As my being expanded, I felt the wonder of the Lord's creation and how my ego mind limited me from understanding the very existence of magic and miracles in which we dwelt.

Learning:

I experienced the weight of the armour we carry. In a process yesterday, I felt my husband's armour not just outside his body but also underneath the skin. When parts of this invisible armour melted, it cut through, giving intense pain. I realised as our armour melts, the raw wounds are exposed and healed.

I discussed my realisation with my husband—how we sometimes freeze our emotions and thoughts thereby numbing ourselves into pseudo-peace. In this denial and depression we shut ourselves out from the world. As we

continue to get scared of things which we find too difficult to cope with, our pseudo-protection gets heavier and
becomes harder to break. We fear the opening of Pandora's
box, which contains emotions we choose not to confront.

When the ice breaks, we head for a life collision; the floods
and the daggers become too painful to escape. By processing, Reiki, meditating, *simran* (repeating the *shabad*),
yoga, and other healing ways, we allow the process to be
gentle. By observing and listening to our body, we can
begin to live a lifestyle that assists the process of purification and that results in the removal of armour.

So how can I help a person who does not choose to live
life? Without the waves, how can we feel life? Armour
numbs us, killing the moment before it's given a chance to
experience the joy in the breath of life. So we postpone living by setting an arbitrary goal to reach; only then will we
give ourselves permission to be at peace. But there are
many rivers to the ocean; likewise there are many ways to
enlightenment. The light of Truth is so powerful that it
can melt the ice daggers before the illusion of pain is too
severe. When we go within and take one step towards our
source, that source takes one thousand steps towards us
and helps us remove emotions, toxins, and lies one at a
time, only giving us what we can handle. This process takes
time; after a lifetime of protection and conditioning, we
have prevented and numbed ourselves from feeling our
pain.

7 February. Day Thirty-eight

The frost made the stars and waning moon seem brighter. The moon scattered its glistening glitter joyfully to celebrate this day. The crinkly waves on the lake looked like patterns of three-dimensional house roofs-triangles intertwining in a myriad of shapes. It felt as if the waves of thoughts were captured and frozen to reveal their Truth. My whole body felt exhausted as if iced into immobility. I felt overburdened by the baggage of thoughts; a part of me wanted to sleep through them so I could blanket any challenges in reality. I felt my mind wanted me to thrive in illusion so as to avoid the underlying issue.

In the distance, across the ice lake, I saw the shining silver swans. I felt a deep connection of love, respect, and wonder. In awe I felt them looking deeply at us with gratitude, yet they could not reach the bread on a physical level.

The fives swans and I fed each other with a deep love from the Oneness in the beat of our hearts. No ice caps or oceans could distance this embrace of divinity. My body melted in deep stillness. I experienced no matter how many pilgrimages we attended, or how many seas we crossed, unless the ego mind is seen and purified, the body remains unwashed.

Harjinder Kaur Chohan

Learning:

I realised how my mind loved the drama and mistakes others had made, how it was reluctant to forgive and rejoiced in its hierarchy in condemning the lies and misfortunes of another person. I had so many faults of my own, yet recognised how my mind wanted to keep this fire burning so that Truth could be hidden and God's love distanced. My mind wanted to keep me separate from my self; just like the ice, my mind rejoiced in thickening and ingraining its message. No matter how hard the water and no matter which colours camouflaged the earth, Truth still revealed itself; its love was so deep that in trust and honour it rose above everything and touched us. Love melted distance and ice.

These forty days of pilgrimage are nearly over. I realised that during this time, my blood was being purified. With this, my mind was becoming absolutely crazy, trying to hold onto the limiting beliefs, such as anger and betrayal. My mind whispered softly, 'Oh, how could you be the victim again; how could you give them another chance?' My insane mind had no resolution in trust; it continued to poison and deceive me with its lies. This very mind was keeping me separated from the infinite mind that would take me to the highest Truth and love of self, which had the power to control everything in the universe with ease and flexibility. I observed this mind was not allowing me to surrender into the beauty and call of nature and God's breath that resided in me.

Inevitably, changes occurred within. As I surrendered into the Truth, I realised this pure gem of a moment was untarnished and untouched by any mind games. My mind released its hold on me and I fell into the ocean of peace once again. I observed how the ego mind was so petrified of dying, it had put a lid on the light of Truth. By fermenting its dramas into repetitive explosive nightmares, it took the juice out of each moment, filling it with devastation instead of celebration.

In seeing this Truth, I realised my blocks were being released. This pain was not the doing of anyone outside— it was the mess I had accumulated in the reactions to my karma. Now I was ready to love it to death, embracing it as it melted into freedom. I was ready to face all my debt, denial, and fears which I had seen in my reflection and taken as those of another. I finally surrendered to my errors of the past and released my failures to the light.

I realised before we cross the seven seas, we need to surrender and open the doors of the five senses, without resistance, letting them pass through without anchor. Once surrendered the Lord will carry us across the final ocean of Oneness, to home. Once lies are burnt by the flame of enlightenment, we will be whole, boundless in freedom and dancing in Truth.

Harjinder Kaur Chohan

8 February. Day Thirty-nine

Walking in the countryside towards the lake, the covering of snow just bewildered us. Once we climbed over the gate and walked upon our platform, it took my breath away. I wished my eye could capture this fresh, unique scene on a camera for everyone to witness. Except for the edges, the whole lake was covered lovingly with pure whiteness. There was a large beautiful circle. I could feel the drumbeats of my pulsing, radiating heart. No birds were here, yet I could feel this swan whiteness awaiting us.

Learning:

I realised if we were not ready to receive a holy bath, the Lord could easily freeze the seven seas. I experienced the seven oceans were within us; in the seven parts of our body—two legs, two arms, one torso, neck, and head. If we had not opened and purified these seven oceans in the body, what purity would we find across the oceans anywhere in the world? Everything we need is here. It all starts from within. Do we wait until the body is frozen in death? The seven chambers within our body receive one common thing-our breath. How close are we to this purity? Are we going to allow the ego mind to separate us from the purity of life which is in every breath?

I experienced the power of the number seven, as I experienced the simplicity of the seven chambers of our body. In Christianity there were the seven days of creation; Jesus chose the number 490 = 70 x 7 to represent the perfection of forgiveness. The seventh heaven was the day of rest. The Cardinal Articles of Faith in Islam are seven, and they say in Supreme Mathematics, the number seven represents Allah. The seven colours of the rainbow were formed from one pure, white light. I realised in Sikhism the number seven is the same sound as in the word Truth and can mean conclusion or completion. *Sath* (seven) also is part of Satnam (true name). Truth is our identity; it also came in *satsang*, a congregation of lovers of Truth. This Truth has no language, it is the Now. I also realised there were seven chakras in our body.

My awareness opened into the colours, the game of life where the Lord gave us clues for us to deepen our understanding of the Truth. These clues for the treasure hunt were designed to take us closer to our treasure chest of God consciousness. In this we find freedom. I could feel the glory of this whiteness. It signified unity of all the colours of the rainbow and chakras. No longer did my eyes desire colours; all colours had become one. God is One; in this all nations, religions, creeds, and colours are united.

This spray of marvellous snow was God's play. I felt His voice saying everything is His; this entire world belongs to Him, and thus all is sprayed with His holy name. I realised in my mind's control of life, my race had got faster, and I became exhausted, leading me into a foggy mist of confusion.

I realised I owned nothing; as I was evolving, even my

Truth was always changing. By owning something, I was saying, I need it; then I would have the fear of losing it, creating a battle, and thus increasing the competitiveness of my mind. By sitting back, opening deeper within, and letting grace carry me, I experienced this effortless freedom. God's breeze of trust made life so easy and simple. In this simplicity there was gratitude in everything coming my way. God was performing all the doing, giving, and receiving. I just had to sit back and admire it all. In this space there was nothing to learn, nothing to improve-these were just ploys of the mind. Just as the snow was everywhere, a pure celebration of loving nature, whatever is here is only God taking from or giving to God. There is no me in form or personality—just freedom.

9 February. Day Forty

This early morning at 5.30 a.m., I experienced an infinite blessing, a treasure in the beat of every new breath. I could feel its celebration and dance in my heart as each breath entered. In the stillness of this breath, I was connected to the whole of creation, and my being bowed in tremendous gratitude as one consciousness of God's love.

Climbing over the gate was like walking into Narnia or Alice's Wonderland. The snow glistened and sparkled on everything, and every branch and bud just held it softly like delicate ice cream. The sky was grey and the brisk air was filled with minute flakes of glitter. The silent lake was mushy with blackened snow around the banks. A beautiful sketch of a duck was carved in the snow by the fingers of the silent breeze. Our seating place was covered in this flurry. The mist prevented us seeing beyond the lake. The scenic view of white, brilliant snow was like a still, beautiful meditation. We had entered through a gate into pure silence and stillness.

Learning:

The distant cars travelling in both directions were similar to the noise of the mind, rushing backwards and forwards from the past to the future, omitting the present. The ego mind, with its all-important news, tried to take us away from this pure silence within. The grey mist only allowed us to meditate on the present; we could not see behind us or further than the lake. We realised this present moment was home. Home was in the very breath we were in, in that very moment. I realised the lake rested in this Truth. When I rested in myself, in this home, the lake, I experienced peace beyond measure. The moment was so rich in Oneness. There was no future or past, just what was here now. The moment was real; everything else was an illusion. When I truly felt this, without a thought or anticipation of what might be, I felt warmth, love, peace, and freedom, and all that I had searched for was present in that moment. I realised that Truth was only present in the moment. This Truth of permanence never changes. We cannot postpone or put conditions on this Truth. When trapped in the ego mind, we can only flick into the past or future. This newness and freshness of the lake was a unique treasure embracing me in the moment.

10 February. Day Forty-one

I deeply thank you Lord for our forty-day pilgrimage. I feel a prayer in every breath repeating your sacred name (*simar, simar hur pul Gobind*). In this is my freedom. I am free in this moment.

The lake was a permeable, mushy sponge layer. A passer-by threw seeds onto the lake. The birds made circles in the air before they landed to collect the seeds; the birds supported each other in their flight. In congregation they all sat on the ice opening their seeds in *satsung*. I watched the birds walk, run, and fly. We humans, land animals, are limited with our body; we can only stand, lie, or sit. Yet with our infinite minds we can take ourselves from our finite beings to fly through boundless dimensions, through time and space. We have the unlimited ability to create machinery to take us beyond the depths of the oceans and heights of the skies. Yet, so easily we absorb our limitations and put the lampshade on our eternal light.

When in the company of lovers of Truth, saints of this world, we can create strength to form circles which can take us away from the illusions, lies, and dramas, to see the bird's-eye picture through God consciousness. We can experience this kingdom of Oneness, God's love and Truth in creation.

These forty days have given us a gift of Truth each day. This journey has taken us deep within ourselves, where we have experienced God's love and wonder and awe of this world in which we are a small part. We cannot save, be true to, forgive, or free another if we do not save, be true to, forgive, or free ourselves first. We cannot meet God if we do not surrender in trust; for it is when we are falling God catches us. In each breath we are given wings of freedom.

Today I went to visit my husband's brother in hospital. His bones were brittle and he could hardly hear us. I gave him Reiki, held his hands, and chanted this month's prayer. I realised there is nothing to us really. This body is temporary, yet it is in the temporary we get lost. I prayed his transition would be peaceful. What is permanent eventually finds us and takes us home again to its Truth in Oneness. If only I could stay awake to this deepest gift of breath and with this true companion, my body, BE the beacon, to bring all parts of me closer to my very self, into Oneness.

Harjinder Kaur Chohan

Epilogue

Somehow, there is nothing to say and yet so much has happened. These forty days were only a beginning. It is December now; a year of pilgrimage has passed. I believed I was beginning this pilgrimage to help my family heal. Yet, I realised, as my ego insanity shed its lies, everything in my life has always been for me. Just for me. My family was just a reflection of my thinking mind, coming to heal my karma which I had created. Today I realise there is no one out there but me—my Self in all its glory, Oneness of God consciousness, my Self in all its boundless, unconditional love, and freedom. God and I are One.

Inside me is a deep stillness, a deep silence in which my soul bathes. Like the sunrise it forever rides the oceans, land, and sky. My journey is growing ever deeper—opening, widening, and suffusing in love. I have awoken from a deep sleep, and sometimes as I process, I go back from this open awareness of Oneness to this physical state. Yet I know my deep operation of processing is going to allow me to open wider, and this divine journey will end as my beloved spirit will eventually consume my conditioned mind. All I will sense will be one love for all. I have witnessed land, ocean, and sky seamlessly become one. When my mind, body, and soul can consistently become one with spirit, God, source—many names for the divine-my soul will give birth to guide me to my destiny, to the pathless path in the here and the now, experienced as forever one.

I bow to and honour you for reading this journey. We are all free, one in God's love. I open my arms wide to embrace you and hold you close to my heartbeat and to tell you I am with you every step of the way in your pilgrimage. Every breath, every movement is a pilgrimage until it joins into Oneness.

My deepest prayer is that we all live this pilgrimage, honouring and being present to this holy existence in which we take every footstep. May every footstep be blessed with consciousness of God's love, freedom, and Oneness. Let us be forever united. Let us walk this pilgrimage together, receiving and freeing each breath into a celebration of glory, wonder, and gratitude.

With my heart so open wide, I hold you in its love forever where trust and Truth reign. So chant with me the songs of our soul, may every thought, word, and action come from this place of universal love. Let us all finally become whole, knowing at last we can give ourselves permission to let go. Just relax, trust, and play, knowing the hand of the creator that created this mould is holding us, breathing through us, moving us in dance on life's playing field.

　　　　Harjinder Kaur Chohan

26 February 2009

Dear One,

On my pilgrimage many deep, profound experiences came to me, stayed for quite a while, and eventually dissolved. It was only through the awakening of this pure state of consciousness that this 'I', associated with mind and body, dissolved enough for the universe to open its heavenly curtains to reveal a deeper, ultimate Truth—Satnam.

The cosmic joke is that this emptiness is what we *already are;* everything inside it is born to die and return to this original state of purity. Every concept and belief that follows a thought of the personal 'I' keeps us suffering and separate from our Oneness. This personal identification has separated us from our Truth for lifetimes. The mind is a lost child in the fairground, obediently protecting this 'I', yet blinded by its sensory desires, distracted by the diversity of forms, ornaments, colours, technology, food, tastes, clothing, scenes, holidays, and so fourth. Whilst playing with the toys in the room, it has got attached and distracted, forgetting to notice the space and stillness in which it resides. Once realizing that we are this space and stillness, we begin to truly enjoy knowing that the toys and objects are temporary. Nothing touches anything; no mind or body can touch another. Only this awareness, this life force, this divine love touches itself in this stillness. We have to come out of the mind, the 'no-mind' space, to be able to truly see the mind itself. Only then can we use the mind as the tool to work for the highest good of humanity, all life, earth, and beyond. We cannot continue to be a slave of the mind; time has come to be the master parent of this lost child. Humanity has to evolve and work from this place of Satnam to create, nourish, and nurture pure divine love into everything, respecting everything from its very core. Only from this place of 'no-mind' can awareness dance, flow, and sing through us, awakening others from this lifetime of sleeping and dreaming.

It is wonderful to have a desire of freedom and a desire to purify the mind. Yet there can be a subtle veil of personal 'I' covering the diamond of the Self. In this space you can become good at manifesting what you desire, yet for searchers of ultimate Truth and Oneness, this veil has to be lifted. Likewise, a robot, looking like a human being, can be an imitation of the human form, yet not the human form itself. The personal 'I' can be purified and life becomes comfortable and at ease, yet there will still be a subtle division, a yearning to stay in an experience rather than be one with all.

There comes a time in this conscious development when all experiences, no matter how noble or worthless, distant or near to the enlightened Self, are just experiences. Pain and pleasure are just experiences-two faces of the same coin. The Self has always been here, yet we have always been missing **the obvious.** But by being detached to both pain and pleasure, we can sit in this ultimate bliss in which the dance is celebrating and congratulating its glory.

The mind is so used to doing a job and making things complicated so that its 'I' identity feels it has done something grand. Yet Truth is simple, free, pure, humble, ordinary, and unassuming, without an 'I' entity. Practices are good; they can allow you to become committed and disciplined to finding this Truth. But remember, the personal 'I' mind loves practices and rituals. So to be vigilant is ever important. You are only on the boat on the river when you begin to go inside this mind and look at it. This requires staying awake. Be on watch, be a lifeguard. There are many methods which can keep you alert enough and create pranic energy for you to be silent and still for the innate awareness, Self, to reveal itself to you. When that happens, remember thought might come in to analyse this experience; stay alert, do not follow it, stay open, stay free, stay looking at the mind, at no cost let it consume you again.

Eventually, to reach the ocean you have to let go of any practice. The boat no longer will serve you. You have to trust and fall in and be totally immersed, otherwise the ride on the tides will continue and the attachment to the boat will get stronger. Ultimately the boat (body) too will leave you. In the ocean, awareness will be your pure state of ultimate Truth.

One has to inquire the most important question of all questions—who are you? Who is experiencing the practice? Who is reporting back that experience? Practice can be a subtle disguise behind which the personal 'I' ego can hide. When we find out who is witnessing it all and even let go of that, no personal 'I' can exist. In this emptiness of no 'I' identity, joy, laughter, bliss prevail.

Reading the book *The Truth Is* by Papa ji, I felt his presence and as I talked to him, he told me, sharply to 'Wake up!' I woke up from this dream state. A deep realization opened its doors to me. Although the experiences I had during the pilgrimage allowed me to become closer to the Self, these eventually faded, and the grip of the personal 'I' pulled me out of myself. Even though immense purification had taken place, there was still an 'I' which somehow owned the experience. In subtle silence it was enjoying doing a good job and making me feel it was me that was experiencing this deep peace and Oneness. It was imitating this ultimate Truth whilst keeping me believing in this space. It was indeed a cleansing state towards pure consciousness.

Only after stopping the pilgrimage did I realize, although the stillness had come and awareness had given me the taste of pure consciousness, once coming back into the 'I' identity, ego wanted to take subtle ownership of this. This 'I' was faint and manipulating, its layers of identification were diminishing, yet it still wanted to be kept alive; it was even speaking in spiritual terms.

Only when the trees become bare in winter, can one see the ivy, the parasite that needs the tree, yet subtly time after time sucks the life force. Likewise, the ego 'I' is feeding off you; it is using you. Once it knows it cannot bark to get your attention it will grow gentle, simmer, stay low, and remind you your desire is being accomplished. Just watch out; it is not your friend; this symbiotic relationship can be the one veil between you and the Self. Why settle for an imitation of the cloak of bliss? Why not BE the pure, eternal, consciousness that you are at your permanent state? In that space you are untouched by the highs and lows of life, for you are beyond the form and mind.

I value and am extremely grateful for all my experiences of the past. They were precious signposts and stepping stones to this awakening. They allowed the purification of the mind and allowed the body to process so true flowering could take place. However, I had to go in and inquire deeper to let go of very subtle notions, beliefs, practices, and experiences.

In awakening, Papa ji made me realize my illusions were like the dreams from which I awoke every morning. In the sleeping state nothing was with me, the unconsciousness was fully awake and I was in this place of Oneness. One particular morning, like a sudden opening in my heart and a flash of lightning in my head, something lifted and opened. In this nothingness, every single particle of 'me' could see and feel as pure One consciousness. There was nothing in me to which anything could grab hold.

Walking up the stairs, I instantly saw the illusion of my home. I recognised that everything was a past thought moving in front of me in this dream; there was no personal 'I' walking up or down the stairs. This awareness moved through everything in such effortless, flowing lucidity, in transparent peace and stillness. There was no reporter. There was no one experiencing anything. Illusions dissolved. It can not be explained in words; it carries no knowing or longing to be known.

Later, for three days tears flowed—nothing happened, in immense sadness, they just flowed. The grief from carrying all the illusions fell away and love poured into the void. Attachment from outside and inside melted. As I walked through my home, something met my son's gaze; our eyes met in Oneness and for the first time ever, there was *nothing between us*—no knowing state. It was the first time I had seen the eyes of one devotional love without me or him getting in the way. In this state there was no mother or son, just this pure, scintillating love, an awareness of Oneness.

When there is no personal 'I', there is no truth or lie-just nothing. That is why it is so easy to be in this state, yet to describe even words create duality. In this state there is so much peace because no one is acting or reacting. Anger might come, but without holding onto the anger and feeding it, all that has happened is movement—change and return to emptiness—Oneness. Experience happens, yet 'I' in Truth and Oneness is untouched by either sadness or happiness, because those emotions are arising out of the bliss of this state.

This, here in the now, has always been here and will always remain. Stillness remains nothingness until a thought arises, then movement is created, and a dance follows. There is no good, bad, or indifferent. Who is there to say that anyway? When silence happens, it is pure silence; even words are just movements which happen in this. In this stillness, there is nothing; it just is divine.

Let go of your notion of 'I' and just be this love that is nameless, formless, still, and quiet. This state will move you and give you a show that is remarkable. Just watch it without touching anything.

Enlightenment is not a place we need to get to; it is our present, pure state of consciousness. We do not need to search for what *we already are.* Every night we are reminded of this very essence in which mind sleeps and the infinite 'I' awakens. Once waking and associating with the personal 'I', we forget the very awareness we have been. All of life happens in this stream of consciousness. This consciousness is Truth—just Truth.

You are this primal state. In this state there is no need for me to give you another experience or understanding for the personal 'I' to engage in. In every moment we change. We are never the same from one breath to another. Without the personal 'I', there is no learner or learning. I am not here to give you further knowledge to collect. You already are this sacred wisdom. I am here to say: The personal 'I' that once had a face and footsteps has dissolved. Thoughts will arise, but no longer am I a slave to them. Nothing came. Nothing happened. Nothing remained. You and I are closer than your heartbeat and your breath. In fact we are one. We are the ultimate, universal Truth. Satnam.

There are many different religions, spiritual practices, and many people who follow truthful, peaceful teachings. Yet those who search sincerely for Truth, no matter what practice is being used, enter the boat and a river. All rivers are going to the same source—the ocean. Once in the ocean you cannot find the separate rivers—all identities fade. Once in the ocean all become one. All which is born from the ocean will return back into the ocean. In truth, nothing was born and nothing died; it was always just an ocean. The awareness is untouched by any moment, colour, sound, or form. It transcends through and loves everything as one because everything is created inside it.

Feel your body fully alive; feel the love vibrating in its core. Share it, feel its dance flowing from the fountains of Truth, touching itself again and again. In the presence of this body, awareness will come in again and again, caressing itself, kissing itself through the whispers of the breeze until it resides forever as Oneness, giving itself away, flowing, hugging, and joining in all that IS as itself in this one Truth.

Who has been walking? Physically? Emotionally? Mentally? Spiritually? Where to?

Stop.

Who are you without the body, the emotions, the desires, experiences, and the mind?

Stop.

Who are you that is witnessing your answer?

From a tiny seed the largest tree was born. From a thought the world was formed. You are beyond power and the creator of all. Once your form was born, you learnt to walk. When walking will cease, you will return to a place of stillness—inside your Self.

Trust the sages, saints, angels, and spiritual teachers. Although language is different, the ultimate words and messages are the same.

Find out who has been walking. Where are you going? From where did you obtain the feet? What came before feet?

Be still. Be quiet.
Stop sleeping. Stop mind walking.
Wake up!
There is nowhere to go.
You have been around and around only to come back to the place
You started from.

Remove the feet of the thoughts that are walking in the past or the future.

Be still. Be here.

The feet cannot leave footprints in the *NOW*. In the now feet are still. There is no distance between you and freedom.

Take away 'you' and take away 'freedom'. What remains?

Here it is.

Enlightenment is your natural state, not an experience to obtain.

Where did you ever go to? Stop the search. You will return to the same space you started from. Return now. Be still. Be quiet. Be nothing. Just for one minute, do nothing.

Be here in the now.

Do nothing.

No-thing.

That which witnesses the sleeping, waking, dream state is pure consciousness. Let go of everything you ever knew. Trust.

Fall.
Fall open.
Fall awake.

In awareness words cease. Self is that which is witnessing even the thought of 'pure consciousness.' Do not get engrossed in the words.

All words are sounds. All sounds vibrate. All vibration

comes out of stillness.

Be silence.
Be stillness.
Be the selfless Self.

Footsteps in the sand are washed away by the ocean. We are walking in the air, in space, from molecule to molecule. There is only the NOW. Even that is gone as soon as you have noticed it.

Be still. Be quiet.

Where are your feet? Be aware.
Sense them NOW.
Start a conscious pilgrimage. Begin here.
Look down at your feet. This is where the journey begins.
Come back home. One by one, turn on the lights, clear out the cobwebs, release the prisoners, forgive from the mind, forgive from the heart, forgive from the soul, forgive again and yet again, forgive yourself.
Open your heart to receive forgiveness from others.
Walk consciously.

Walk into freedom. **Walk into Oneness.**

Acknowledgements

I thank the Gurus, and I thank The Holy Granth Sahib and its teachings. I thank all my teachers: Papa ji, Yogi Bhajan, Brandon Bays, Byron Katie, Karta ji, Hari Har ji and other great teachers. I thank you for choosing to read this humble script, thus experiencing a part of my journey.

I deeply thank my husband, Tarlochan, who walked, prayed, and chanted with me in the early hours of the morning each day for one and one-half years. I also thank my sons, family, and friends for supporting me. I thank my friend Elspeth Jane who gave me a retreat in Wales whenever I needed to be silent and still to help me process and purify. I thank Jane for her hospitality, help, and her love of nature and photography.

This book is in honour of my late Grandma Bachant Kaur who taught me the love of walking, listening to her stories at bedtime, and chanting prayers during the day and before sleeping. It is dedicated to my Grandad Sadhu Singh who taught me the love of words; he loved reading the dictionary. I honour his patience and excitement in seeing me coming home from school, his reverence, gentleness, and deep trust in me. I am grateful to him for seeing **me** before I ever knew myself. He was such a good listener, and he taught me to never look above at those people who had more than me, but to look below and **feel gratitude** for having so much more than so many in this world. I thank him for choosing my name, he had taken a half from both parents, 'Har' from my dad and 'inder' from my Mum. It is only when I felt its vibration, its meaning lifted me. Hari - Guru, Jind - Life, Dar - door, translated as 'the door to Guru's life'. This book is a tribute to my Nana ji Niranjan Singh who always saw the goodness of my spirit and his love just flowed for me; he taught me the value of strength, dignity, and honesty. He gave me his most precious pen which he was awarded in honour of his service in the Gurdwara in Canada.

I thank and honour my Mummy ji, Surinder Kaur, who has taught me the most valuable gifts in life: integrity, endurance, the gift of valuing and nurturing everything I have, the gift of Truth, punctuality, early rising and sleeping, having a balanced meal, valuing water, clothes, and so much more. Her daily practice of prayer and service and her courage to rise above adversity by seeing the bigger picture is a powerful gift to the mind in times of illusion. Her life of simplicity and value is what I want for myself. It is her consistency in giving all these states of Truth which capture and hold me.

I honour and thank my spiritual mother, Bibi Gurdev

Kaur, who has increased my love and understanding of Sikhi. I am grateful for her devotional *keertan*, teachings, and the power and vision one mother can hold—giving strength and purpose in raising self-esteem and consciousness of so many Asian women in this country and beyond.

I honour and thank my Daddy ji, Harbhajan Singh Aujla, for his life of virtue, value, stability and adventure and for taking assessed risks. I thank both my parents for always being there for me and supporting me fully all my life.

I honour and thank my father-in-law, Pyar ji, Udham Singh, for his patience, stories, riddles, love, and trust in me. I thank my mother-in-law, Bibi ji, Surjit Kaur, for the care of my children, tidiness, courage in her later life, living through dialysis, her deep trust in me, and for teaching me patience and of how the mind and its games can control and imprison us.

I honour and thank my wonderful brothers, Jagrup and Balraj, for always trusting deeply in me and giving me endless love and respect, and for always listening and standing by me and seeing my light even in my darkest hours. I thank my brothers and their beautiful wives, close to my heart as sisters in Oneness, Harjinder Bhabi ji and Mandip, for their deepest respect, trust, adventure, joy of walking, hiking, travelling, love, care, and so much support given unconditionally to me and my family. I thank their children for their kindness, humility, simplicity, playfulness, love, and for sharing so much laughter with us as a family.

I thank my dear sister Parveen, who taught me sign language and the preciousness of my senses. Through her I learnt how to listen to the sounds of nature and observe its beauty. At the age of eight I prayed deeply for a sister, and I realized how God gives what we ask for in sincerity. She became the catalyst that allowed me to talk to God and to hear His whispers in the breeze around me. It is only now I realize there is no bridge outside between God and me; God is inside me, underneath the voice of the commentator of my mind, in the soft, loving whispers of life which move me. I thank her husband, Dave, for his creative talents, inspiration, confidence, and courage to live life to the fullest.

I thank my sister Jarnail and my niece Kieran for their courage, strength, and stamina to survive adversity and come out of it like shining stars. I thank Jarnail's wonderful family and especially Daman for her delicate, soft words and for always embracing me with her love.

I thank my late aunt Davinder Pureval who died at the age of thirty-seven. During those thirty-seven years she believed so much in me. She gave me so much hope, love, and reassurance in times of need. She was my anchor, inspiration, my friend, and sister.

I thank my spiritual cousin Rani in Canada, my loyal cousins Meena, Pumi, and Sukhi and their wonderful children. I thank my uncle Mohan Singh for his high expectations as a Principal in India, Malkit Singh for our special walks and his beautiful letters, and my late uncle

Gurbax Singh for our special pilgrimage to Hem Kunt in the Himalayas.

I thank my beautiful angels, Iris and Helen, who helped me at university. Without all their patience, care, support, time, and love I would not have been able to accomplish my teaching degree. I am deeply grateful for my friend Philipa who was a parent of two of the pupils I taught at school. She came at a time in my life after our house fire and my deep depression. She just knocked on my door with flowers in her hand and would come and do reflexology on my feet. It began to open and release something inside my body. I thank her for being my angel who came to help me begin my journey within. I went on to do complimentary therapies and consequently my healing work got its name 'Heel 2 Heal'. I am forever grateful to her for being such a beautiful soul in my life.

I thank my lifelong friends Manju and Bryony, my spiritual Reiki brother, Steve, and all my relatives and friends I have not mentioned here for being in my life and holding me in their hearts as I hold them. There have been, and still are present, many other great-uncles, great-aunts, and relatives who have been great inspirations to me. In your hearts you know I mean you, so I thank you deeply for sharing your breaths with me.

I thank all my teachers and staff I have worked with in schools. I thank all my Reiki, Kundalini Yoga, and Journey family. It is an endless list. If we are one, names only separate us.

I thank my son Sarandip for his love, forgiveness, gentle caring nature, and for playing with his brothers and looking after them when he was younger. I thank him for his patience, for the company he has always given me, and for his courage and vision of hope in challenging times. Last year he got married to his beloved beautiful wife, Ninderpal, the wonderful, caring daughter I finally have beside me. I thank her for choosing to share her life with us and for joining us to her wonderful, caring family.

I give thanks to my wonderful, brave son Amardip, who with courage and patience has risen from an adversity that left him very still for a few months after an accident last year. When he lay on the bed in a different country, shock and guilt came pouring through me, as I had brought him here and given him this gift for his twenty-first birthday. We found out he had broken his back and shoulder. My son, who had just completed his sports degree was here now reminding me of my back injury. I sat beside him on the bed alone that night; he could not close his eyes as pain absorbed him. In surrender and stillness, I sat in the quietness. I asked him what was he fearing? Like a five-year-old child, he cried, 'I can't close my eyes Mum, I'll never be able to sleep again in my life; all I see is that quad bike coming towards me, this time its going to kill me.' This is the son who loved the outdoors, who loved living life to the fullest. In the stillness of my soul, I heard the words speak from silence through me: 'Die son, close those eyes and let it kill you.' Without a question his eyes closed. In that moment I knew there was no mother and no son. The voice came again and instructed, 'Die son. Die.' He closed his eyes and died. I asked, 'What is here now?' He replied, 'Relief' and his face softened. Something had released him. I repeated, 'What is here now?' and he replied, 'Gratitude.' Tears came and his voice spoke in beams of love and blessings. In surrender and humility he whispered, 'I am so happy Paramdip is okay, and it's just me who's hurt.' So much love poured out of him. Just love. Tears of gratitude overwhelmed him. In that embrace of divine blessings my son slept serenely. So what had died? Ego. Mind and the thought of fear in which it resided. 'Amardip', his name means eternal light. He had returned to that openness, the space from which we can never die or be born, for we are forever one.

I thank Amardip for his love for nature, and his excitement for life and adventure. When he was younger he was able to take me back to my childhood and allow me to reclaim this loving energy again. I was privileged to see in him such pure brotherly love and sharing at such an early age. It was a miracle watching Amardip save his biscuits, cakes, and sweets for his brother Sarandip. Sarandip had always talked to him during my pregnancy; he spoke to Amardip before his limbs were born. This immense love Amardip had for him was a pure joy to watch. A language beyond words was transmuted there before these two brothers met in flesh. They also are so close and Paramdip just loved sharing with Amardip.

I thank my beautiful youngest son Paramdip, who turned

twenty-one years of age last year on the thirtieth of November. He wishes to give, to serve and improve the health of others through medicine, although he and I often debate over how much medicine has to do with no-mind and awareness over matter. I love your humour, Paramdip. I love all the times you melt me with your loving kindness, all the times you played the violin and sang to me.

I love you sons, all the times we have hugged, cuddled up together, and laughed. I love hearing, watching, and feeling you get on with each other, and play and laugh. I forgive you for breaking my ornaments whilst playing cricket inside the lounge. I loved your school cooking days, the days I could free myself and enjoy eating what your little hands cooked for the family. I thank you for all your wonderful words in cards. I cannot believe you all are men, yet in a blink of an eye, I connect to the child in you all-or is it the innocent, bouncy, pure love that was never embarrassed to express itself? This expression of Truth is ever flowing, yet this Truth is unchanged.

I thank you sons for choosing me as your mother, for giving me such glorious times, for seeing your stunning plays—Joseph, Shakespeare's Midsummer's Night Dream, Romeo and Juliet—for seeing your drama acts in town, your football, cricket, and tennis matches, and for the holidays we shared. I thank you for the laughter and fun you have had together whilst I have just sat back and watched in awe and gratitude of all my blessings bestowed upon me.

Goodness, I must have created some good karma to have had such a privileged life, with such love given to me, with such joy and laughter and sons who have always brought me happiness, peace, humour, and harmony. Thank you to my beautiful Ninderpal for the beautiful voice with which you say 'Mum' and your hug that just melts me. I thank the other two daughters yet to come. This book is dedicated to you my children.

May everyone's life be filled with this ambience of joy, peace, and Oneness. Just turn around, become aware, feel yourself breathing, your heart pulsating, look into the light, and count your blessings.

Let us not talk about love, but be the source of love. Let's share the greatest treasures of its expression which flow through us today: our smiles, warmth, touch, kindness, appreciation, words, creativity, and so much more. The seed of a flower is planted, and the journey begins towards the stem that grows and carries us. Rest comes; in that surrender the ultimate flowering takes place. In all its stages of this journey, perfection is here, in the travelling, flowering, disintegration, returning, and distribution of seeds into the soil, to create again and again. We are all recycled incarnations with one common denominator. Find it. Thoughts will come and go, emotions will rise and cease, but once your permanence is found, you will forever be true to Truth, flowering in every breath, in every gift of life, and knowing that everything around you comes from the same seed, same origin, sharing this same earth as one humanity.

Appendix

I was given the following shabads from the Sikh scriptures. I was told we would receive a gem after each month of chanting them. At the end of the year we would receive a gift of immeasurable value.

JANUARY 2007

Asa Mahala 5

Bhai prapat manukh dehuria

(Oh Man!) you have been given this human body

Gobind Milan ki eh teri baria

Your time has come to meet the Lord of this world

From (Rahras Sahib, The Holy Granth Sahib) Shabad translations are taken from 'Sacred Nitnem' by Harbans Singh Doabia

An additional message from **Being** was also written for each month:

You are a precious Divine Soul, celebrate your existence. Each breath is a pearl that unites you to the pure diamond within. Open and expand. Your limits are boundless. Be in bountiful gratitude, so you may manifest your abundance this year and forever more.

FEBRUARY

Nhat phirio lie sat samundran

Those who take baths in the seven seas
(all places of pilgrimage)

Lok gayo parlok gavaio

Without God's worship, lose this World
as well as the next one

(Savaiye, Granth Sahib)

Additional message:

You can keep searching but what you are looking for is at your doorstep. When you are at peace in your Home where Spirit dwells, all treasures will be yours and the search will end. Rejoice—this breath is your key to the switch, which will light up your home and you will see it as if for the first time. Welcome Home.

MARCH

Namastang anile, Namastang anade

I salute God, who has no colour or form. I salute God who has no beginning.

Namastang achhede, Namastang agadhe

I salute God, who cannot be broken. I salute God, who is unfathomable.

(Jaap Sahib, Granth Sahib)

Additional Message:

You can desire material attributes, possessions and external beauty, yet it will all fade. It is temporary—reach out for what is permanent. Your Truth and liberation is beyond the physical realm. May the fire of enlightenment burn the lies of the ego mind and allow your potential to shine through you—for the infinite mind is God consciousness.

APRIL

Ik Onkar Vaheguru ji ki Fatah, Patsahi 10 (Dasvin)

God is One. Victory is of God. The Tenth Satguru.

(Savaiye, Granth Sahib)

Additional Message:

We are all United, all One big family. We will all surrender to the will of God one day. So why not surrender today and trust the wings of faith to lead you to forgiveness and freedom.

MAY

Gur Kirpa te se jan jage,
jina Har man vasia, bolah amrit bani

Those, who wake up, keep God in their hearts by the Grace of the True Guru and utter Nectarian words.

(Anand Sahib, Granth Sahib)

Additional Message:

So remain awake during night and take each breath of life to obtain that what is real. The dramas of this world will entangle you in the net of prison. Wake up to what is Eternal Truth. See the bigger picture.Learn from the lessons. Find the gift and move on.

JUNE

Gavai ko gun vadiaia char

Who can sing the virtues and excellences of God?

Gavai ko vidia vikham vichar

Who can sing and describe the most difficult
knowledge of God?

(Jap ji, Granth Sahib)

Additional message:

Singing makes the heart grow bigger, chanting mantras
increases the vibratory frequency in the mind. This flow
harmonises and releases chemicals of joy for us to feel the
juice and wonder of life. Happiness is lived as Heaven on
Earth. We become our authentic Self. Hum, sing, chant
with a smile.

JULY

Ja tis bhana ta janmia, parvar bhala bhaia

When it pleases God, a child is born and then
the family loves it

(Anand Sahib, Granth Sahib)

Additional Message

Maya is the influence by which God is forgotten. Attachment suffocates and moves love away. Detachment frees and moves love closer. God's name opens your heart and lets you Be Love.

AUGUST

Satnam

His name is True

Karta-purakh

He is the Creator

(Jap ji, Granth Sahib)

Additional Message:

United we can create mansions, yet the natural creations of the Lord are magnificent. Take a vacation; see the places of natural beauty. Walk in day and admire the stars at night. You might be lucky enough to see a shooting star.

SEPTEMBER

Asa mahala 1

Akha jiva visrai mar jao

I live when I repeat the Name, I die when I forget it.

(Rahras Sahib, Granth Sahib)

Additional Message:

Let this dance of life be a continuous prayer of gratitude to the support our body gives us. Be in awe and reverence of all that we have. Accept this is all that we need at this moment.

OCTOBER

Salok Mahala 1

Dukh daru Sukh rog bhaia ja Sukh tam na hoi

Pain is (becomes) the remedy, while joy (of this world) is (becomes) the disease. When there are (worldly) pleasures then (human being) does not love God.

(Rehras Sahib, Granth Sahib)

Additional message:

Is pain or pleasure two faces of the same coin? Who knows what contracts we have made? Who knows what gift pain can bring? Who knows if pleasure is freedom or a trap? Trust your intuition, a neutral place where 'I' and 'mine' does not exist.

NOVEMBER

Alik hain, Nnsnk hain

Nobody can portrait God, God has no relatives

Nrisrik hain, Asanbh hain

God needs no support, God cannot be understood.

(Jaap Sahib, Granth Sahib)

Additional message:

I keep an invisible bucket in my head, all the whys, negatives and all the unknowables go in the bucket. Thoughts are like seeds, be careful, be conscious of what you are planting.

DECEMBER

Garab ganjan dust bhanjan mukat daik kam

God destroys the ego of the proud and is the destroyer of the evil doers. He confers salvation and fulfils desires.

(Jaap Sahib, Granth Sahib)

Additional message:

When the lake is still the reflection is clear as a mirror. Likewise, when the mind is still, Truth is revealed. In that is one's meditation and serene peace.

Stop playing small, take the lampshade off and let your true potential and creativity shine through. Be innocent and let your diamond radiate. With humility the four doors of the Universe will open and bow to the United Love and Light of Grace in You. Be in Satsang (company of lovers of Truth).

(Adi Granth) 'Listen, you messengers of death; do not go anywhere near a Saint. They are always absorbed in meditation, singing the song of God's praise. Neither of them can escape, when they enter the sphere of a Saint, a Lover of Truth'. So my friends be in this company of <u>Truth</u>.

A Daily Reminder

Make this day yours by being present to THIS MOMENT. The river flows and in every moment it is a new river. Live in the flow—the past is a lie, the future not here yet, only what is here is Real. This breath, this abundance is on loan, PRAISE THE LORD for this RICH moment. Feel, breathe, taste, drink LIFE. Celebrate Now!

Harjinder Kaur Chohan

Printed in the United Kingdom by
Lightning Source UK Ltd., Milton Keynes
141003UK00002B/2/P